PREACHING WITH POWER

Sermons by Black Preachers

Edited by
BISHOP JOE ALDRED

CASSELL

Cassell

Wellington House, 125 Strand, London WC2R 0BB

370 Lexington Avenue, New York, NY 10017–6550

www.cassell.co.uk

First published 1998

British Library Cataloguing-in-Publication Data
A catalogue record for this book is available from the British Library.

ISBN 0–304–70439–3

The sermon 'Skin deep Christianity' by Reverend Ian Sweeney on pages 39–43 also appears in *The Fourth Times Book of Best Sermons* (Cassell, 1998).

Typeset by Keystroke, Jacaranda Lodge, Wolverhampton
Printed and bound in Great Britain by
Biddles Ltd, Guildford and King's Lynn

CONTENTS

ACKNOWLEDGEMENTS

This book of sermons has been made possible only with the goodwill of a number of individuals. My thanks go to Gillian Paterson at Cassell for responding to my initial verbalizing of my vision for such a publication, and for her patience in working with us on this hitherto uncharted road. Special thanks go to Pauline Foster for her role as project co-ordinator, which has become a euphemism for the person who has had to do almost all the work. Without her input it is doubtful whether this project would ever have been completed. Thanks also to Jayne Byrne and Diana Hardiman, administrative secretaries in the Centre's office, for their assistance. And of course, a very big 'thank you' to our preachers who have been willing to 'expose' their manner of sermonizing to a wider audience than that preached to in the first place.

INTRODUCTION

Preach the word, be urgent in season and out of season, convince, rebuke, and exhort, be unfailing in patience and in teaching.

(2 Timothy 4:2 RSV)

I recall the first time that I, from a Black Pentecostal background, was invited to preach in an Anglican service. During the finalizing of the arrangements for my visit, I enquired about how much time I would have to preach. The minister, without a hint of irony, informed me that I had seven to ten minutes. 'Seven minutes?', I retorted in total disbelief, 'in my Church the greetings alone last that long.' That encounter epitomized the ignorance which historically has existed between different Church traditions in Britain. Ignorance which it is hoped that this compilation of sermons by Black preachers will contribute to some degree to dispel.

The Bible posits the question 'how will they hear without a preacher?' The issue of preaching is taken seriously by Black Christians everywhere as the primary means by which the Gospel is communicated. Every week, on Saturdays, Sundays and during the week, in prayer meetings, regular services, conventions, convocations, seminars and crusades, Black preachers are at work expounding the Gospel to whoever will listen. Understanding the Gospel as the power of God unto salvation, liberation and freedom, they preach with the urgency of 'a dying man to a dying world'.

The contributors to this compilation come from across the denominational spectrum. No attempt has been made to restrict ourselves to those Churches which are generally called Black-led or Black-majority. Black preachers practise their art, their calling in White-led and White-majority Churches also, and so the reader will find them also here.

Black is used here in the politico-cultural sense to include Africans, Caribbeans and Asians, some born here in Britain, others born abroad and resident here.

These sermons, or messages as they are called in some Churches, have been preached already in various settings and are replicated here, having been duly adapted by the preachers for this publication. The reader will find sermons of varying lengths and types, sermons of contrasting, sometimes conflicting, doctrinal positions. We have not striven for consensus.

There needs to be an awareness that Black preachers rarely confine themselves to reading a sermon, and so some imagination is necessary on the part of the reader. Replicating the 'call and response' and the general preacher–congregation dynamic is virtually impossible in print.

My prayer is that this will be a catalyst for many more publications from Black theological practitioners in Britain, and that this and other literary contributions will assist the process of the development of mutual respect between different Christian and non-Christian groups through greater understanding and appreciation of who we all are.

Read, enjoy and be blessed.

Bishop Joe D. Aldred, Editor
Director, Centre for Black and White
Christian Partnership

THE WAY FORWARD

Reverend Ronald A. Nathan

For twenty years, Reverend Ronald Nathan has served as a pastor, missionary, teacher and community consultant in the Caribbean, Africa and the United Kingdom. He was ordained by the Pentecostal Assemblies of the Caribbean and is an Associate Member of the Progressive National Baptist Church (Europe).

Until recently, Ronald was the Director of the African and Caribbean Evangelical Alliance (ACEA), Britain's largest Black Christian networking and development agency. At present he is a freelance lecturer and consultant and is reading for a Master's degree in Applied Theology at Westminster College, Oxford.

Ronald hails from Trinidad and Tobago and is married with two children.

KEY SCRIPTURE: PHILIPPIANS 3:13–16

Our title today forces us to look to the future. It anticipates our involvement and it works for transformation. This has always been intrinsic to the Christian gospel, because it draws on the lessons of the past, it makes sense of the present, and it moves towards a positive engagement for the future.

The text allows us the space to re-interpret its message from a first-century urban context to our complex advances in information technology and their own inequalities. From Philippi to London, across the centuries humankind is faced with choices of eternal proportions. These would impact our knowledge of God, knowledge of self and knowledge of our role in society.

As people of colour living in Western society, we have been bombarded with images that state our past was irrelevant, our present existence is grudgingly tolerated, and our future is dependent on the favours of others. God never designed His people to live without hope in this world or in the next. There has to be a way forward. One that will not result in our people abandoned to the scrap heap, eating the leftovers of an affluent nation.

The Christian must be aware that we are in the world and therefore linked into the social, economic, political, cultural and religious realities of the day. These verses of scripture cannot therefore be relegated to the issues of the 'spiritual' only. We must know Jesus Christ within the sphere of the whole gospel, for the whole person, for the whole world.

To know Christ (verse 10) leads to conformity to Christ (verse 15), and gives the impetus for attainment through Christ (verses 14 and 16).

Dr Ray Bakke, who has written about urban mission, points out three things that restrict the Christian from rising up through Christ:

1. Lack of information
2. Lack of motivation
3. Feelings of intimidation.

Although there are many committed members within our congregations, the negative impact of the above factors has had a telling effect upon our own Church's witness. The logic and reasoning behind the first factor is 'I don't know'. The second, 'I can't do it'. The third, 'It has never been done this way before'.

The first is based on ignorance. God's word says 'I would not have you to be ignorant' (Romans 1:13). The second is caught up in a dependency syndrome. God says to *you* 'I can do all things through Christ who strengthens me' (Philippians 4:13). The third reveals a fear of the unknown. 'God has not given you a spirit of fear but of love, of power and a sound mind' (2 Timothy 1:7).

The apostle Paul refused to give the first-century Philippians an 'opt out' clause from Christian living even in the desire for a heavenly home. We too must take his words seriously in our post-modern, post-Christian society: 'this one thing I do, however, is to forget what is behind me and do my best to reach what is ahead' (verse 13). This verse must never be misunderstood as a command to abandon your culture or even the traditions of the past. It is a call to reject all those things that would restrain your efforts for moving ahead. In my own experience I have discovered that a knowledge of Black and African history has supplied me with resources for the future.

Paul's encouragement to press on is a clarion call to those who feel trapped by past disappointments, failings, abuses, stereotyping and lack of opportunities. Let's press on! Let's move forward, in our knowledge of Christ, in conformity to Christ, in attainment of Christ-centred goals. Let's move on from the unemployment queues, the police interview rooms, the admission centres of mental institutions, the victims of police brutality, the poverty of substandard education and housing, and the drug dens of our inner cities.

It would seem to me that if the Apostle was with us today in the United Kingdom with its multi-racial, multi-cultural, and multi-religious population, he would look at the popular British pastime soccer, and draw at least four lessons for our progression and move forward:

1. Keep your eyes on the prize
2. Run with the ball
3. Be a team player
4. Stay within the rules.

First, keep your eyes on the prize. If the Black Churches are to lead the Black community out of the predicament that it is in, we must focus on the prize of self-help, self-development and self-sufficiency. This is not to disparage or hate any other people. We cannot hitch our hopes for a better life on the willingness of others to give us a piece of the cake. This is to fulfil the biblical injunction encapsulated in the phrase 'God blesses the child that's got its own'.

Church, today I want to say to you that any religion that is not interested in your total liberation is an oppressive religion and should be rejected. Religion has become a drug in our neighbourhoods. We have enough religion to get us to heaven a billion times and back, but none that is prepared to get us a job, to build us a factory, or to provide decent and affordable accommodation.

The prize of the high calling is not just the populating of heaven in the sweet by-and-by, but also the depopulating of the hell we call slums, disease-infested housing, the psychological pain of racism, and the demotivation of life without any hope of employment. The abundant life promised in John's gospel does not begin at the time of death – it has to begin at the point of life in Christ.

We must keep our eyes on the prize. We cannot afford to be side-tracked by theological gymnastics such as the moves against the ordination of women or the divisions of denomi-nationalism.

Secondly, run with the ball. The footballer that runs down the left flank at full speed, gets before the goal and shoots without possession of the ball, would be the laughing stock of the stadium.

The Christian who indulges in worship on Sundays, prayer meetings on Tuesdays, bible study on Thursdays but avoids the realities of the homeless, the infirm and the HIV/AIDS victim is running without the ball. The gospel is 'people-centred', not programmatic. It is still the power of God unto salvation and it must be allowed to transform lives. We are running without the ball if we fail to understand the link between a faith decision (salvation) and popular decision-making (politics). To preach prosperity without seeking to eradicate social injustices is to run for goal without the ball. If our church pews are full and we ignore the plight of those in full prison cells, then we are truly running without the ball.

The gospel is not simply a call for conversion, it is a call to a lifelong commitment to truth, righteousness and justice. It is the transfer of allegiance from one team to the next. It includes lip, life and literature, what we say, how we live and what we portray in written and artistic form. The gospel is creative, we cannot separate our music from our experience of spirituality. We cannot separate our economics from our prayers and we cannot separate our Saturday Schools from our children's education.

Jesus in his manifesto (Luke 4:18) reiterates that the Good News is good news to the poor, captive, blind, down-trodden and the disenfranchised, all those who feel they have no stake in society and are spoken of as expendable.

Thirdly, be a team player. One player cannot win a football match. The more individuals in the team that play their part, the greater the possibility of success. The more we invest in people, the greater the recognition that all people are created in the image and likeness of God. They are filled with God-given gifts and need to be treated with love and respect. That is how we nurture potential.

The gifts of the Church have to be put at the disposal of the community. Many times we within the Church fail to remember where we came from, that had it not been for someone else, we would not be where we are today. Yes, we were on drugs and using our body to get money to feed ourselves. We gambled the wages and drank the night away. But God . . . somebody say *'But God!'* bowed down from on high, found us on the underbelly of society, got messed up so that we could be cleaned up. Now we are too holy to offer a homeless child a home or to give a pound to help that person sitting outside the train station.

The gifts of the Church must be offered to God and placed at the disposal of our communities.

Our young people must be moulded with the teaching of Christ-centred values. 'Train up a child . . . ' the Bible says . . . would someone help me this morning! What legacy are we leaving for our offspring when we live selfish lives, not caring for anything else but keeping up with the Joneses? With our Christian respectability intact, we do not play as a team.

Our young people must be motivated to do good works. They must be mobilized in the pursuit of greatness. They must be allowed to rise above mediocrity and second-classism. As a pastor, I was determined not only to have a good choir and extensive real estate. I recognized that God had placed within my sphere of influence bundles of potential that would need motivating to take up positions of importance in society, not just in the choir. I realized I was shaping lives for leadership in the service of Jesus Christ. We must encourage debating clubs, science projects, and career development, alongside conventions and convocations. Most Black Churches do not celebrate Black History Month; then we wonder why many of our children leave the Church in their teens and claim that Christianity is a white man's religion.

You may not want to say 'Amen' but it is true. Where are your children this morning, brothers and sisters? Let's motivate them to good works. We are not the only players. Clergy cannot do it without the laity. Men cannot do it without women. Youth cannot do it without the elderly. The choir cannot do it without the administrators. The evangelists cannot do it without the prophets.

Fourthly, stay within the rules. In every game there are rules; if we do not abide by these whatever our skill, we will be excluded from the game. A personal relationship with Jesus Christ cannot be divorced from the responsibility to build healthy relationships within our communities. Obedience, humility, holiness, righteousness, love, joy, compassion, and kindness are non-negotiable commodities of the Christian life.

The cliché that is used is that 'the anointing breaks the yoke'. The yoke of oppression must be broken by establishing institutions and structures that are based on the principles of the Kingdom of God. Prayer and advocacy must work hand-in-hand.

Attendance in church must provoke us to punctuality on the job. The tenth commandment, as summed up in loving the Lord with the totality of our being, must be seen in our love towards our neighbour. Spirituality must not be reduced to a set of dogmas and denominational pronouncements. Liturgy must not point only to a future glorious age, but must relate to the present condition of the worshippers and their deliverance.

The way forward for the Black Church must be as an agent of education, a model of motivation and a venue of security and stability. It is such a Church that would regain and hold the respect of our children and point them to the 'Way Forward'. Amen.

A NEW WORLD

The Right Reverend Doctor John Sentamu

The Rt Revd Dr John Sentamu was born in Uganda in 1949. He was educated in Masooli Kyambogo and Kitante Hill, and Old Kampala School, Uganda. He studied law and worked as a barrister before becoming Chief Magistrate, then Judge of the High Court of Uganda. He was arrested for his criticism of the Amin regime for human rights violations. This led to his later departure to the UK. He studied theology at Cambridge, receiving his doctorate. He was ordained in 1979. He was Vicar in Tulse Hill between 1983 and 1996. He was a member of the General Synod of the Church of England from 1990 until becoming Bishop of Stepney, serving on numerous subcommittees, working parties and groups. He is also a member of numerous national and local bodies, a regular speaker on radio, television and conferences. His priority as Bishop is to seek God's rule of justice, righteousness, peace and love.

KEY SCRIPTURES: PSALM 96; LUKE 22:7–20

Prayer: May I speak in the name of the Son, in the power of the Holy Spirit, to the glory of God the Father. Amen!

To speak on the theme of this Holy Communion Service (Greenbelt Sunday Communion), A New World, fills me with such joy and excitement because the subject matter, given by our bible readings, is so close to my heart. I feel like a boy who stood on Liverpool docks, that great port of the slave trade, and observed slaves unloading molasses from the West Indies. The sweet smell almost intoxicated him. The crane kept on lifting sacks of molasses above the boy's head: he longed for a few drops. Suddenly one of the sacks burst and the boy was covered from head to toe in syrup. Underneath the syrup he was heard praying 'Lord, give me a tongue worthy of the task'.

We are this morning treading on holy ground, given the mighty downpour of last night. Rain in Africa is a sign of blessing, and perhaps my prayer should be 'Lord give me a tongue worthy of your praise!'

Why am I excited by the theme of our service? Simply because of the context of our mission today. Most people in Britain clearly know what *not* to believe, but very few people have a clue as to what to believe. The Enlightenment gave values and meaning to the missionary context and enterprise — but today those values and the context of mission have changed. The Enlightenment emphasized the role of reason, which would give us an objective *value-free* knowledge leading to a clear understanding of cause and effect, and indeed the purpose of our existence. This led to the optimism of *progress*: the future would always be better: we can therefore modernize, because all our problems in principle are solvable. The individual, therefore, is *autonomous*. These theories, however, are no longer believed, and on the streets of modern Britain these ideas are no longer *practicable*.

People today in Britain are reaping the Enlightenment harvest with the result that most people have a radical doubt about everything. You name it, they doubt it. Ours has become a culture of contempt; and everybody, especially the media and the press, has been to that graduate school of demolition and has passed with flying colours, with PhDs to their name (PhD = Pull her/him Down). A good example of this is the A-level and GCSE pass rates: up a quarter per cent year on year. Reaction? Not 'Praise God', but 'there is a continued worry that exam papers are too easy and standards are slipping'. Had it been the other way round, I suspect this would have been blamed on poor, ineffective teachers and the poor motivation of all pupils and justifying the need for league tables. Idle childlike behaviour in the market-place, as our Lord calls it. 'We played the flute for you and you didn't dance; we sang a dirge for you, we wailed, and you didn't weep' (Matthew 11:7).

Institutions of stability and authority have been greatly undermined. Everything has been reduced to a commodity culture and there is a general feeling of rootlessness all around (politicians call it 'the feel-good factor'). Hence, the call for clear leadership, clear authority, and definite beliefs — perhaps so that even these may be pulled down.

Although it is clear to everyone that not all problems are solvable, there is still a reluctance to believe that there are many problems we do not know the answers to. More than a decade ago, Graham Clay, now Principal of Ridley Hall, Cambridge, prophetically said:

> There is a real sense in which the Western world has lost a definite sense of the past. The future is filled with uncertainties and people are living in a perpetual present; and being terrified of the present, they fill it with commodities. Shopping has become the primary cultural present of the Western world in the twentieth century. And this cultural present has even invaded Sunday.

Creativity is no longer what we *make* or *think* but what we *buy*. The uncultured are those who cannot enter into the cultural present of our twenty-first-century world. The truism of the Enlightenment, 'I think, therefore I am', has been replaced by the consumer culture, 'I shop, therefore I am'. My importance in society is measured by the size and contents of my shopping trolley!

The individual perceived primarily as a consumer now means that churches try to put on what people can buy into. So people are made to search for spiritual experiences and *gurus* endowed with the gifts of 'making it happen'. The result is people shop around for a church that will uplift them and not necessarily the one that will radically change them into Christ-likeness. *Consumers of religion and not real disciples of Jesus Christ.* And churches are looked upon as take-aways:

the choice between Burger King, Kentucky Fried Chicken, etc. And of course you may choose to go to a Mega-Church: Harrods-type, rather than the Woolworth-type down your street. And so the culture has become a matter of style and taste. What matters today is what things *mean to me* and not whether they are true. Graham Clay again said that Western culture today can be described like children visiting a shopping mall sweet-store: a culture of *pick 'n' mix*. A plural society with great problems and great opportunities and yet unwilling to face up to the challenge of relativism that has invaded all areas of Western society today.

Into that British maze the Psalmist in Psalm 96 says 'Praise the Lord, the King'. Yes, a new outburst of song because of a new event that evokes it. The Lord is so great and his works so wonderful that it takes 'all the earth' to do justice to such a theme. The greatness of this God as Creator and Redeemer is so compelling that the Psalmist must utter vocal musical praise. The thought of who God is kindles the fires of devotion to the point where praise cannot be restrained.

In verses 1–3, the Psalmist is so excited about God's offer of salvation, peace, wholeness and a worldwide transformation, transfiguration (which will come through the impending judgement of the Lord), that he must tell it to the ends of the earth. It is a change that gives joy to the world, which is so extraordinary that it can only be ascribed to the divine intervention.

A new world order is being ushered in by the greatness of the glory of the Lord and the greatness of 'his wondrous works'; therefore this knowledge is something that the nations need to hear and would indeed gladly receive if they but heard it. The chief point at issue is that, if one truly grasps the greatness of our God, that makes that person vocal in letting others know what great things the Lord has done for them and is ready to do for others. 'A beggar telling other beggars where to find bread.'

Any reader of the New Testament soon discovers the great difference between present-day Christianity and that of which we read in the New Testament. The difference is that to us it's primarily a *performance*, to them it was a real experience.

We are apt to reduce the Christian faith to a code, or at best a rule of heart and life. To these early Christians it is quite plainly the invasion of their lives by a new quality of life altogether. They do not hesitate to describe this as Christ 'living in' them. Mere moral reformation will hardly explain the transformation and the exuberant vitality of the lives of these early Christians — even if we could prove a motive for such reformation, and certainly the world around offered little encouragement to the early Christian. We are practically driven to accept their own explanation, *which is that their little human lives had, through Christ, been linked up with the very Life of God.*

Secondly, I want you to remember the fact that the New Testament was written, and the lives of the early Christians, caught up with the Good News of God in Jesus Christ, were lived, against a background of paganism. There were no churches, no Sunday Services, no Greenbelt Festivals, no books, no tapes, no Website of the Faith. Slavery, sexual immorality, cruelty, callousness to human suffering, the treatment of women as household goods, and a low standard of public opinion, were universal; travelling and communications were chancy and perilous; most people were illiterate — no wonder God so loved the world that he didn't send a fax or an e-mail. But came in a human person: Jesus of Nazareth, who has bound himself forever in a covenant of love in his life, death, resurrection, ascension, and the outpouring of the Holy Spirit.

Many Christians today talk about the 'difficulties of our times' as though we should have to wait for better ones before the Christian faith can take root. It is heartening to remember that this faith took root and flourished amazingly in conditions that would have killed anything less vital in a matter of weeks. These early Christians were on fire with the conviction that they had become, through Christ, literally sons and daughters of God; they were pioneers of a new humanity, founders of a new Kingdom. They still speak to us across the centuries. Perhaps if we believed, we might achieve what they achieved. The Psalmist is excited about the greatness of God as Creator, because this means that every power in the universe is subject to God. And by God's grace the power of God can be made manifest, God's rule of mercy, love and justice made visible. The Psalmist is excited about the glory and greatness of God because he clearly sees God as Redeemer. This took centuries to be realized. St Paul in 1 Corinthians 15 reminds the Corinthians of the essence of the Gospel:

> And now let me remind you (since it seems to have escaped you), brethren, of the Gospel — the glad tidings of salvation — which I proclaimed to you, which you welcomed and accepted and upon which your faith rests; and by which you are saved, if you hold fast and keep firmly what I preached to you, unless you believed at first without effect and all for nothing. For I passed on to you first of all what I also had received, that Christ, the Messiah, the Anointed One died for our sins in accordance with [what] the Scriptures [foretold], that he was buried, that he arose on the third day as the Scriptures foretold.

This historical basis of our faith is of crucial importance. We need to hold on to it and not try to build a superstructure of spiritual experience. When the Jesus 'trip' fails, then people abandon faith because it was just another trip. For the New Testament Christians the fact of Christ was the unshakeable reality even when things were going disastrously wrong. The *fact of Christ's person* — that he was and is the Son of God; the fact of Christ's death and resurrection — these facts are the basis of our faith.

We are saved by the one who upholds the universe. As Paul says in Romans 8:28ff.: 'Nothing can separate us from the love of God in Christ.' It is the fact of Christ, which answers the cries for today: cries for meaning, purposes of life; where can significance be found? Or the cry for love? The Number

One problem of today is loneliness. Or the cry for freedom, for forgiveness. The answer is Jesus Christ who died for our sins and rose again and offers his Holy Spirit to all who believe in him — and who lives in his body, the Church.

This is our message of a New World order. The risen Lord in Luke 24:45–48 helps the two confused disciples on the road to Emmaus to stop groping in a smog of confusion and despair.

> Then he [thoroughly] opened up their minds to under-stand the Scriptures, and said to them 'Thus it is written, that the Christ, the Messiah, should suffer and on the third day rise from the dead, and that repentance [with a view to and as the condition of] forgiveness of sins should be preached in his name to all nations. Beginning from Jerusalem. You are witnesses of these things.'

Witnesses of these things: which things? — the death and resurrection of Jesus Christ and the offer of forgiveness to those who repent. The greatest gift the Gospel of Jesus Christ offers is the forgiveness of sins. You can never do anything bad enough for God not to forgive you if you come prepared to turn around and let God be in charge — be in the driving seat of your life. When you come like that He puts your sins in an indestructible box without a key, buries it at the depth of the sea, and a signpost goes up: 'Fishing Prohibited.'

New Christians are made by Christians made new. The covenant of love offered in Christ relates to experience. Those who are to transform the world must have a first-hand experience of the foretaste of the power of the age to come. In 1 Corinthians 15, the Gospel of Christ is not just in accordance with Scripture, but the living Christ appeared to Cephas, the 12 to 500 other believers all at once, and James and also to *me*, says St Paul.

Nothing shuts the mouth, seals the lips, and ties the tongue, like the poverty of our own spiritual experience. We do not bear witness for the simple reason we have no witness to bear. At my tenth birthday a friend of the family came to my party. He said if I gave my life to Christ, there would be a big party in heaven. God, all the saints and angels will really rejoice that I had asked God to come in my life. Before I went to bed I prayed 'God, if it's true that you will be really happy if I give my life to you, then please come in my life. Amen!' The next morning I told my mother that I was sorry for the times I had not been kind and co-operative. At school I told my dad, who was the headmaster, that I was sorry for taking four exercise books and giving them to the other boys so that I could get banana pancakes during break-time. At the end of the school day, during final assembly, he called me forward — I confessed, and was severely caned for my wrongdoing. You know the best decision I have ever made was to ask God the Holy Spirit to come into my life. Life has not all been easy but I know the difference Christ has made and is making in my life.

Verses 4–6 of Psalm 96 give us the reason why the Psalmist is so full of joyful praise. The God the Psalmist rejoices in (and who is made manifest in Christ and has called us to be his friends by the death and resurrection of Jesus Christ) is *greater than all those that people want to call gods. The reason for praise: God's incomparable greatness.* Because God's greatness and his praise inevitably go together — one can't consider the one without breaking forth into the other — this naturally implies that the fear his knowledge evokes is wholesome and true: it's a godly reverence. God's creative work of the universe ought to keep impressing us with the greatness of its Creator. Strength and beauty are often separated in a disordered world, and each is maimed thereby, but in their perfection they indissolubly blend. And this greatness of the Lord is offered to us in the making of the new heavens and the new earth.

And what should our response be? In the words of the Psalmist in verses 7–10 of Psalm 96, 'let us ascribe to the Lord the glory due to His name'. In everything we do let us act in such a way that clearly recognizes the nature of the God we adore. Let us approach in the spirit of deepest awe, that is to say, 'tremble before him'.

Archbishop Desmond Tutu tells a story, when he was a religious knowledge teacher in a primary school in Soweto, of a boy who gave an interesting answer to a question during an exam. The question was *'When Jesus came to be baptized by John the Baptist, what did John say to him?'* The boy answered *'Now that you know you are the Son of God, start behaving like one'*.

The trouble with many of us, we behave like a hyena that followed the smell of the roasting of a goat. He followed the smell pretty well until he came to a crossroads. He turned his nose to the left and the smell was great. He turned his nose to the right and the smell was great too. He kept playing ping-pong with the smell for several hours and eventually the smell died out and the poor hyena never got anywhere near the roast. This morning the Lord is calling you and is saying, stop behaving like that hyena. Come and he will lead you. Now that you know you are a child of God, start behaving like one.

The Lord is King of all the earth. This truth will save you from stumbling about blindly. This will also give you insight into the whole world and its government. For if God reigns, then the world is established and it shall not be moved. For God's government is effective and adequate in every detail. The knowledge of this truth is essential for that sense of security that people so badly need. God shall judge the peoples righteously. So what joy and satisfaction to know that the administration of the world and its affairs, from the perspective of God in eternity, are in competent hands, and that there is no possibility of God failing in any respect in the work that is rightly his.

A new world order will come to pass. The process was set in motion with the birth, death, resurrection, and ascension of Christ and the outpouring of the Holy Spirit. Each time that thought arises, there ought to be an occasion for gratitude to God, for all created things are involved in that great divine restoration, and all should, therefore, contribute their portion to the vast chorus of praise that should continually rise to heaven because of this great prospect. And that's why the Psalmist in verses 11–13 of Psalm 96 calls all created things to praise God:

> Let the heavens rejoice, and let the earth exalt; let the sea roar and all that fills it. Let the field exalt and all that is in it; then shall all the trees of the forest shout for joy before the Lord, for He comes, He comes to judge the earth; He will judge the world with righteousness and the peoples with His truth.

And this judgement, like on Calvary, delivers many, offers forgiveness, new life and a new creation. As St Paul puts it: 'Anyone in Christ: new creation! Everything old has passed away; see, everything has become new!' (2 Corinthians 5:17). A day is coming when what is true of the individual will be true of the created order. A New World.

Oh yes, we may go through trials and tribulations now, but the Lord of the resurrection is here and the dawn of a new day is breaking upon us. He is using our experiences of failure, pain, and sorrow mingled with joy to weave his masterly tapestry, the underside of which is always a tangled mess and the topside which is always beautiful. Like Good Friday: ugly, cruel, messy; and Easter Day: glorious, bright, joyful, victorious. The two sides are needed. We are God's work of art.

President Nelson Mandela put it beautifully when he said:

> Our deepest fear isn't that we are inadequate. Our deepest fear is that we are powerful beyond measure. It's our light, not our darkness that most frightens us. We ask ourselves, 'Who am I to be brilliant, gorgeous, talented, fabulous?' Actually, who are you not to be? You are a child of God. Your playing small doesn't serve the world. There's nothing enlightening about shrinking so that other people won't feel insecure around you. We were born to make manifest the glory of God that is within us. It's not just in some of us; it's in everyone. And as we let our own light shine, we unconsciously give other people permission to

do the same. As we're liberated from our own fear, our presence automatically liberates others.

The world looks for better methods. God looks for better men and women, changed by the Holy Spirit promised because of what God has done in Christ Jesus. Have you signed up yet? Have you got on board yet?

But please note. This call to sign up is not for joining a Sunday School picnic party or the last of the summer wine, but to war for the well-being of our human race. Like the famous battle cry of Giuseppe Garibaldi (1807–1882):

Soldati, io esco da Roma. Chi vuole continuare la guerra contro lo straniero venga con me. Non posso offrirgli nè onori nè stipendi; gli offro fame, sete, marcie forzate, battaglie e morte. Chi ama la patria me segua.

Men, I'm getting out of Rome. Anyone who wants to carry on the war against the outsiders, come with me. I can't offer you either honours or wages; I offer you hunger, thirst, forced marches, battle and death. Anyone who loves his country, follow me. (*Oxford Dictionary of Quotations*, 1981 edition)

Brave hearts joined in their thousands! And what a victory!

This morning I am going to ask you individually to respond. Respond to this God of love who in Christ promises to be with you now and in the new world to come. *Please* stand and hold out both hands and say 'I am coming Lord: now that I know I am a Child of God, I have started behaving like one'. All of us stand and make a festal shout three times: '*The Lord reigns.*'

TRUE WORSHIPPERS

Pastor John Francis

Pastor John Francis is married to Penny, who has supported him throughout his ministry. Over the years, he has become known as a man who has a clear purpose and is willing to stand in the face of adversity. Filled with a vibrant and fresh anointing, this dynamic man of God brings life and restoration wherever he goes. Sharing his vision with the Body of Christ, he challenges us to awake from our complacent stupor and live fruitful and effective lives.

He is the General Overseer of Ruach Ministries, one of the fastest-growing Churches, which is based in Brixton, south London. The Church has grown rapidly in a short period of time, with churches being established around the country. His ministry has taken him throughout Europe, America, the Caribbean and Canada. He has also travelled extensively throughout England. John Francis' ministry can be seen and heard on television and radio on his programme *In the Spirit*.

KEY SCRIPTURE: MATTHEW 15:21–28 (AV)

Then Jesus went thence, and departed into the coasts of Tyre and Sidon. And behold, a woman of Canaan came out of the same coasts and cried unto him, 'have mercy on me, O Lord, thou son of David; my daughter is grievously vexed with a devil'. But he answered her not a word. And his disciples came and besought him, saying, 'send her away; for she crieth after us'. But he answered and said, 'I am not sent but unto the lost sheep of the house of Israel'. <u>Then came she and worshipped him</u>, saying, 'Lord, help me'. But he answered and said, 'it is *not meet to take the children's bread and to cast it to dogs'. And she said, 'truth, Lord, yet the dogs eat of the crumbs which fall from their master's table'. Then Jesus answered unto her, 'O woman, great is thy faith; be it unto thee even as thou wilt'. And her daughter was made whole from that very hour.*

Worship – what does it mean?

Dictionary definition: Reverence and respect paid to deity; adoration or devotion paid to a person or thing; homage; to idolize.

Shachah (Hebrew): Prostrate; homage; crouch, fall down; make to stoop; or worship.

The word 'worship' comes from the Anglo-Saxon word 'worthship'.

In Anglo-Saxon times when pirates went treasure hunting, they would look for treasures of great value. According to what they found of great worth, they would put it in their ship. Hence, we get the word 'worthship'. So worship is paying homage to someone or to a person who we feel is of worth, or valuable.

Now, in Matthew 15:25, the Bible tells us that this woman of Canaan came and worshipped Jesus and said 'Lord help me'. She had already petitioned Jesus and stated her need and had received no response. She was not deterred. She had most probably heard from friends, or in the market-place, that Jesus the man of miracles was in town, and she needed a miracle. In approaching Jesus and speaking to him, she disregarded the protocol of the day, leaving herself wide open for ridicule and rebuke.

There are at least three reasons why she should have kept her distance. First, she was a Gentile; a non-Israelite, a non-Jew, a heathen, with whom the Jews rarely interacted (John 4:9). Secondly, she was a Canaanite. The Canaanites were

Israel's ancient enemies. They were a perverse people, practising temple prostitution and sacrificing children (Numbers 33:50–55; Deuteronomy 7:1–11). Thirdly, she was a woman. For a Rabbi to speak to a woman in public was considered improper (John 4:27). A Rabbi would not even speak to his wife, mother or sister in public.

The disciples even said to the Lord to send her away, but despite the obvious barriers to her receiving healing for her daughter, she still persisted. Jesus' cutting reply should have been enough to put her off. To be told that he had not come to help her, but to help the lost sheep of Israel, His own people, was indeed insult enough. But then Jesus goes on to say that it wouldn't be proper to give the good bread, which is for the children, to dogs! In other words, Jesus was saying, it's not fair for me to take this good healing, this good salvation, this good deliverance and give it to a Canaanite dog.

Jesus called this woman a dog. Despite all this, the woman does not get upset, she does not sweat. There are times when we are insulted, despised, abused and we shout our indignation and injustice from the rooftops. Perhaps what we need to do is to take a leaf out of this Canaanite woman's book. She turned to Jesus and she said 'Of a truth, Lord, I am a dog, but even the dogs get to eat the crumbs which fall from the master's table'. She acknowledged that in the Lord's eyes she was low and considered nothing. Her words touched the master's heart. No matter how low you think you are or how small people tell you that you are, God can make a difference to your situation.

Have you ever watched a pet dog or cat at meal times? They sit patiently waiting for something to fall from the table or for their master to throw them some food or some scraps. 'I am a dog', the Canaanite woman said, but there is something that comes off the master's table that I can have, that I am entitled to. Her remark touched Jesus, knowing that He had ignored her and insulted her, yet she was still waiting and still expecting. Even as a dog, there was a blessing on the master's table that she was looking, hoping for: a crumb, a drop, a tiny morsel of leftovers, especially for her. Jesus acknowledged her, and said 'O woman, great is thy faith, be it unto thee, even as thou wilt, today'. Her daughter was healed that same hour. Through her faith she received more than just crumbs.

Her daughter was made whole.

The woman with the issue of blood, she touched the hem of Jesus' garment. She wasn't supposed to be touching anyone, but because of her faith she was made whole. I know there are some blessings and some wonderful things that I'm going to receive because of faith.

Some of you have had some experiences that would make your mother's toes curl! You have been hurt and abused, or you have behaved in ways in which you are thoroughly ashamed. Some of you wouldn't dare testify and tell where the Lord has brought you from and what he has brought you out of. Today, you are the image of respectability with your hats and your suits, you are all decked out, but you know that you were not always like this. Remember, Jesus is attracted to your sin. He is Holy, but He steps in to cover your sin. The Bible tells us in Matthew 9:13, that 'Jesus didn't come for the righteous but to bring the sinners to repentance'. Also, in Matthew 9:12, Jesus tells us that 'those that are whole do not need a physician'.

However, we understand that when we were messed up, living sinful lives, Jesus was there, waiting for the right time, the perfect moment to change our lives. We know that if it were not for Jesus, we wouldn't be who we are today. We could not achieve holiness by ourselves. It takes the blood of Jesus and the Holy Spirit in our lives to make that difference.

Last year, some of you were in clubs, rubbing 'n' dubbing, or in a promiscuous relationship with a man or woman, but this year you are shouting 'hallelujah'; lifting up holy hands in the sanctuary and blessing the name of the Lord.

People don't understand what has happened to you or what is happening to you. All you know is that you did something, or said something that got the Lord's attention.

I want to take a moment to concentrate on the women.

Often women are made to feel like the underdog, like they are worthless. The scriptures are turned around and used out of context to suit the situation or circumstance. This is due to a lack of understanding of the historical importance, or in ignorance of the important details of the scriptures. For example, telling women they ought to keep silent in the Church is often used as a form of persecution to keep women 'in their place!' Some men wish to keep women down, telling them they cannot do this or that, but there is something about women that is very special!

Men know how to discipline and make rules and regulations but women, women know how to pray! If you want a great revival, ask the women to pray. When they pray, Zion is in travail. When the women pray, they get results. You won't know about 'travailing and bringing forth' unless you are a woman. Only women know about the pains of their monthly cycle. Only a woman knows about Braxton Hicks contractions and labour pains in childbirth. Women don't find it hard to get down on their knees to bring about their revival or breakthrough.

Esther knew what to do when she was faced with adversity. She and her maidens fasted and petitioned God. She dressed and perfumed herself and got herself ready to go before the king. Women, you are powerful, you possess a special anointing. You know how to worship to get God's attention. This is what us brothers need to learn to do: attract Jesus' attention in a way that brings about a breakthrough in our lives.

If you want to get my attention, as a man, I need to be attracted to you. There must be something about you that gets my attention.

Some of you need to start to make an effort and make yourselves look good. Perhaps your husband or wife has left you, or perhaps your plans for marriage fell through. Pull yourself together, you never know what special blessing the Lord has in store for you.

Brothers, we need to learn a few things from the women. They are sensitive and sensible. When it comes to attraction, they have got it down to a fine art. When I look in the Bible, I find that the majority of the times when Jesus interacted with women, it resulted in revivals. For example, the Canaanite woman is one that tapped into Jesus in such a way that she got His attention and received more than just crumbs (Matthew 15:21–28).

Another woman of immoral living, a prostitute, washed Jesus' feet with her tears, dried them with her hair and anointed them with costly oil. Her actions, which by many were considered a public disgrace, moved Jesus to speak to her and send her on her way, her sins forgiven and her faith commended (Luke 7:36–50).

Now, you wouldn't find a man doing something like that! Women know how to open up and share their emotions and their feelings. Look at a man. For example, when he comes to the altar and receives a 'touch' from the Lord, he holds back. He feels the tears coming down but tries to compose himself, stopping himself from letting out his emotions.

It is important for us to realize that it is these very emotions that touch God. God is not interested in your sophistication, your composure and control. God wants to be in control. You are battling, trying to control God, but God doesn't want you to control Him, He wants to control you.

Now, let's look at the Canaanite woman again. The Bible tells us that when Jesus ignored her, she came and worshipped Him. The Bible also tells about David, who was a man after God's own heart. When David messed up, he didn't play the fool, he confessed and worshipped God. He tapped into God. David was a very emotional man. He wasn't ashamed to cry unto God and tell Him the truth about his sin. We know that when someone is broken and crying, no matter how upset you are with him or her, you feel their remorse. After David confessed his sins, he would worship.

So, how do we tap into the heart of God? Through worship. If you have never, ever cried a tear from the time you accepted the Lord, then you haven't pursued God's heart. Remember the Bible tells us that 'a broken and a contrite heart, he will not despise' (Psalm 51:17).

Now let us consider yet another woman of the Bible: the woman of Samaria. She was another social outcast who, according to the law of the day, Jesus should have had nothing to do with (John 4). But on this particular day, Jesus decided it was necessary for Him to travel through Samaria. Jesus stopped by the well at Sychar. His disciples had gone into the city to buy food. Sometimes we need to realize that there are some breakthroughs and solutions that will not happen until we are alone with the Master. Jesus, using the simile of water, introduces salvation to this woman of immoral means. The woman was shocked that this man, a Jew, was speaking to her. But Jesus pointed out that if she realized who was asking her for a drink, she would ask for the living water.

According to the scriptures, Jesus had come primarily to the Jews, His own, but they had not received Him. But as many that would receive Him, He had given them the privilege to become the children of God (John 1:11–12).

That day, this woman, who had five husbands and the one she was with was not hers, was given the joyful task of spreading the good news of salvation. Jesus didn't condemn the woman regarding her past or present lifestyle, but He forgave her and sent her on her way rejoicing. After He had finished ministering to the woman, He made a statement to her saying that the hour will come when the true worshipper will worship the Father, His Father, in spirit and in truth.

God is raising up a new generation of people who, in the past, have messed up, or done something they are ashamed of. However, the difference is, they can testify of their past without reservation regarding where God has taken them from. Just like the woman of Samaria, they will call from near and far, 'come see a man!' He must be the Christ. But now the hour cometh, God is seeking true worshippers, who will worship Him in spirit and in truth. We, as Christians, must worship in the spirit and in truth, in order to move God.

Yes, God is raising up those who are not interested in ordinances and church rituals, but those who will worship Him in spirit and in truth, no matter what. Yes, God is raising up real worshippers, effective Christians who will testify to reach others, those who will tell the truth about their past, their struggles, and how they became victorious. For it is only when we live the truth and worship in the spirit that we can relate to ordinary people and win them to Christ.

Then, and only then, can we be called the true worshippers.

WHAT DO YOU WANT ME TO DO FOR YOU?

Reverend Eve Pitts

Reverend Eve Pitts is a vicar in the Church of England, in the parish of King's Norton, Birmingham. She grew up in Nottingham. After leaving school at 16, she had various clerical jobs and also worked in the Civil Service. From 1985 to 1987, she was the Race worker in the diocese of Southwell, before going to Queen's College, Birmingham.

Eve was ordained deacon in 1989, and then served as curate in the parish of Bartley Green from 1989 to 1992. She moved to King's Norton in 1993, and became an ordained priest the same year. She is a member of the General Synod of the Church of England.

Eve is married with three children.

KEY SCRIPTURES: MARK 10:46–52; AMOS 5:1–17

Jesus was on his way to Jerusalem. This was to be the last time he passed this way. The road was crowded, let's imagine for a moment, with shoppers, mothers, fathers and toddlers. But there was one young man there who could not, even if he wanted to, be part of the crowd. He was blind, and his blindness meant poverty because there was a lack of compassion for him. Many Jews would have believed his blindness was the result of a curse. He may have been a figure of fun and affection, all rolled into one. A lot of the time he may have been ignored. This was daily life for Bartimaeus.

He had nothing to rush around for — he had time enough to listen keenly to what was happening around him. A keen ear was important for his survival. So was the ability to be heard.

Let's imagine how he might have felt when he heard that Jesus was passing by. Perhaps he was frustrated: would anyone hear him amidst the noise of the crowd? How many of us, when we think we are not being heard, have feelings of isolation? Maybe this was Bartimaeus' only chance of meeting Jesus, for Jesus was not likely to pass that way again. This was a 'drowning' man wanting to be saved. And so, he yelled at the top of his voice: 'Jesus, Son of David, have mercy on me' (Mark 10:47). Perhaps he was taken aback when Jesus heard him and asked what appears to be an obvious question: 'What do you want me to do for you?' (verse 51).

My response to such a question would have been 'What do you think I want?' But Bartimaeus could not afford to be sarcastic. 'I want to see', he responded. He took the opportunity handed to him. He received healing. 'Go', Jesus said, 'your faith has healed you.'

This is a story with a happy ending. But life is not always so simple. Who are the people among us today who are crying out? Who are likely to be the Bartimaeuses of our age? The unemployed, perhaps the homeless, the disabled, and many more, I have no doubt. They too are confronted by the daily realities of society's apathy and annoyance. And yet it will be only through their persistence that they are heard, that they will get the recognition they deserve.

In the earlier part of this same chapter, we read of the rich young man who wanted glory without sacrifice. He lacked persistence. Yet Bartimaeus, in his apparent helplessness, craved the healing power of our Lord. Are we persistent enough on behalf of, and with, those who are in need? Are we willing to enable their voices to be heard? What can we do to give voice to those who are voiceless and enable them to cast off those things which bind them, and to have a fresh start? Jesus is as willing today for us to find a new way of living. He promised us in his word that we might have 'life in all its abundance'. I believe this is as true for us today as it was then. Sometimes it will appear that life's experiences can break us. But through our willingness to acknowledge our need, Christ is willing to meet us where we are, and to help us face new possibilities.

A new self-understanding is offered when we encounter Christ in openness and honesty. Jesus responds to our cry. He enables us to make fresh choices to help us to truly live — not as isolated or lonely individuals, but as part of a living community.

Bartimaeus, a poor, blind beggar, found his voice, received healing and wholeness. He learned that our pain can be conquered by God, but only after we have acknowledged that pain. And Jesus, the compassionate healer, brings release. Amos writes 'This is what the Lord said to the house of Israel: "Seek me and live"' (Amos 5:4).

Amen.

THE CHURCH OF GOD

His Grace, The Most Reverend Father Olu A. Abiola

His Grace, the Most Reverend Father Olu A. Abiola (BD, MTh, PhD and Diploma in Biblical and Religious Studies) is the General Superintendent of the Aladura International Church, Chairman of the Council of African and Afro-Caribbean Churches UK, Co-Chairman of the Centre for Black and White Christian Partnership, and Co-President of the Council of Churches in Britain and Ireland.

KEY SCRIPTURE: PSALM 50:5 (AV)

Gather my saints together unto me; those that have made a covenant with me by sacrifice.

What does the word 'Church' conjure up in your mind? Are you thinking of a building or people? Perhaps you are thinking of a typical church building with a tall spire, or with a tower, rather like a castle, surrounded by a graveyard. But the Church existed before such buildings were ever thought of. The first Christians did not have special buildings; they simply met in each other's houses.

The Greek word *ecclesia* which is translated 'Church' means simply, by derivation, 'that which is called out' or otherwise called 'the people of God'. Applied first to the congregation of Israel under the Old Covenant, and such a familiar word to our Lord's own contemporaries, it naturally was used to describe the body of His followers under the New Covenant. The Church is the pilgrim community of believers with the Word of Jesus Christ as testified by the Apostles, as its guide. The Church is the body of Christ and the composition of the Church are the Christians with their varying degrees of talent, gifts, offices, mission and calling. The mission of the Church is to the world and not for herself and that mission is the proclamation of the Good News and the fulfilment of the promise of freedom, justice and peace. The Church remains permanently dependent for the ground of its existence on God's saving act in Jesus Christ, which is valid for all time.

The gospel of Jesus Christ is its criterion — the gospel that Christ proclaimed and to which the Church of the Apostles witnessed. The Church did not come about of itself. God Himself called it into being as the *ecclesia*, the body of those who answered the call, and this He did in the world, from among humankind. God Himself convoked the Church in the call that was issued through Jesus Christ. This call is the Good News: the news of God's love and the dominion of God over this world, the news that the hopes and desires of mankind should be directed to God alone, and of human love for God and all mankind.

The visible Church

There is the visible Church, which is defined as the 'body of people' bound together here on earth by a common faith and common institutions. There is also the invisible Church, which is merely a number of souls known only to God, who have really received with a lively faith the message of the Kingdom — the sum total of all people in the world who are really Christians.

. What I want to concern myself with today is the visible Church of God. The Church is visible as a human fellowship and through its acts as a community, through its preaching and teaching, its prayers and hymns, its confession of faith and its baptism, its work of love and compassion. All the faithful belong to the visible Church of God, and it is clear that it can never be merely a particular class or caste, a group of officials or a clique within the fellowship of the faithful. The Church is always and in all cases the whole people of

God, the whole fellowship of the faithful. Everyone belongs to the chosen race, the royal priesthood, and the holy nation.

All members of the Church have been called by God, justified by Christ, sanctified by the Holy Spirit. And all members of the Church have been called by the message of Jesus Christ to faith, obedience and complete devotion in love. We all belong to the Church through our human decision. Although the Church is decreed by God, it is dependent on free human assent in faith and obedience, as there can be no Church without human beings, just as the Church is impossible without the merciful and loving call and election of God. The Church of God is more than the sum of its individual members, which God has gathered into His people. We are the Church — not God, not Christ, not the Holy Spirit. Without us the Church has no reality. There can be no faith, sacraments and offices, nothing of an institutional nature, without human beings. All these things exist in the fellowship of believers, who are the Church; it is this fellowship, which is identical with the new people of God, which constitutes the basic structure of the Church.

The visible Church of God remains constantly and in all things dependent on Christ, in every moment of its existence, and constantly needs His grace and forgiveness. The Church lives, but not the Church: Christ lives in it.

Position of the Apostles

The foundation of the whole organization is the authority of the Apostles. Apostles are the official witnesses to Christ's resurrection, and they are Apostles because of the fact that Christ's commission was given to them personally. Not gifts of preaching, of organization, not any unusual spiritual experience, not personal merit, but the fact of their having been sent by Christ in this special manner is the basis of the Apostles' authority. It is this group, 'the Twelve' is our Lord's own term for them, which, in the days that followed the Ascension, is found exercising a general authority. They are the centre of all the subsequent developments, the

32

missionary activities for example, the institution of the order of deacons, the replacing of Judas Iscariot, and it is to the Apostles that St Paul submits his claim to be acknowledged as a thirteenth Apostle, 'one born out of due time' indeed but nonetheless of the true lineage.

From the apostolic age the Church has been endowed with authority as its principle of unity. Unity is essential and the source and means of unity is authority, and obedience to authority is the first duty of all believers. Those who exercise that authority decide but do not discuss. Here we have the notion of faith as a deposit, a traditional whole handed on as it has been received, the notion of authority as the teacher, and the notion of these as things willed and instituted by Christ Himself. Side by side with this fact of the Apostles' authority is the believers' realization that together they form a whole, that they are truly a new people although they are of different race and culture. The new doctrine they teach is not offered to the world as a reasoned philosophy. Its teachers do not seek to convince by any argumentation from principles, by any system of proof and deduction. It is presented as an indivisible body of truth to be received whole from the teacher, as he himself received it: and to be so received, not on any personal judgement of the reasonableness of its detail, but on the authority of the teacher.

The birth of the Church

Twelve disciples are summoned to Christ, heralding the reconstitution of the people of God. They are joined with Him in mission, and called to share in the consummation of His baptism as He invites them to shoulder their cross and follow after Him on the mad march to the holy city of God (Luke 9:22, 23, 51). Like their master, they are sent to 'the lost sheep of the house of Israel', for the Lord who commissions them is the one who brings salvation to the seed of Abraham, the divine shepherd who comes to seek and to save the lost. The ministry of Jesus moves towards the gathering of the saving remnant of the people of God, and at its heart stand the twelve disciples appointed to be with Him. It is to the twelve disciples that Jesus turns, as the Last Supper brings the ministry to its close. To them the word of God has been spoken; from them the response of faith, obedience and surrender has been elicited; in them the new community is in process of formation. The Lord alone can bear the sins of the world, drinking the cup the Father has given, actualizing His baptism, the consecration in His blood; only when that sacrifice has been accomplished will His disciples partake of His cup and be immersed in His baptism.

After the Ascension, the twelve disciples returned to Jerusalem and, in fear of the Jews, locked themselves away, while in obedience to Jesus' last commands, they awaited the imminent coming of the Holy Spirit. On the day of the Jewish feast of Pentecost, the Holy Spirit came in the noise of a mighty wind, appearing over each as a tongue of visible fire. And they began to speak in different tongues according as the Spirit gave them to speak. The holy city was filled with pilgrims from every province of the East, from Persia and from Rome itself. The rumour of the heavenly sign spread, the crowds began to gather, and these pilgrims of different tongues understood, each in his own language, what the disciples of Jesus said. Bewilderment seized on them, and anti-Christian slanderers offered their first curiously futile explanation, 'These men are all full of new wine'. The seclusion was at an end; and strengthened by the undeniable miracle, they went forth to announce themselves to the world. Peter preached his first missionary sermon, gathering in thereby the first converts — about 3,000 souls.

Repentance of past sin, belief in Jesus Christ as God and Saviour, and baptism — these are the conditions of membership. For the rest the new group led the life of traditional Jewish piety: prayer, fasting, alms-deeds, attendance at the temple, the breaking of bread, and a practice of voluntary poverty. Day by day their number grew, and the miraculous signs which had supported the Master's teaching followed the work of the Apostles.

The attributes and characteristics of the Church

1. *Unity*: its connecting bond — the indwelling of the Holy Spirit. If the Church consists of those who are united to Christ, and are the members of His body, it is evident that the bond which unites them to Him, unites them to each other. The vital bond between Christ and His body is the Holy Spirit, which He gives to dwell in all that are united to Him by faith. By one Spirit we are baptized into one body, for we are partakers of that one Spirit. The Holy Spirit is the spirit of love as well as of truth, therefore all those in whom He dwells are one in affection as well as in faith. They have the same inward experience, the same conviction of sin, and the same repentance toward God and faith in our Lord Jesus Christ, the same love of holiness, and desire after conformity to the image of God. There is, therefore, an inward fellowship or congeniality between them, which proves them to be one spirit. He dwells by His Spirit in all His members, and thus unites them as one living whole, leading all to believe the same truths, and binding all in the bond of peace. This is the unity of which the apostle speaks in Ephesians 4:4. The Church is one, though she spreads all over the world.

2. *Holiness*: holiness makes the Church a living body, and consequently, the means and agent of its own growth and happiness. The Holy Church stands out distinctly from the world: it does not take its rise from a merely natural development, like the kingdom of this world, nor from the self-development of the spirit of man. God, the Holy Spirit, is the author and principle of its growth. The Holy Spirit, who abides within the Church, is her invisible preserver and reformer, withstanding the encroachments of worldliness; and although particular Churches may lose their spiritual life in the world, the Church herself can never become secularized. Notwithstanding corruption, not withstanding relative pauses and backsliding, the Church holds on her course, and cannot miss her final goal.

3. *Catholicity*: catholicity means the gathering up of all aspects of truly Christian converts with God into a unity of

devotional expression in which every believer can join. The word 'catholic' means 'throughout the whole'. When the Church is so called, it is meant that she is catholic as regards time, place, and faith. Catholicity is an attribute of the Church in regard of these four particulars — its diffusiveness, as being spread throughout the whole world; because it holds the whole truth; because it requires the obedience of all men to all its precepts; and lastly, by reason of all the saving graces given to it. The Church of God cannot be moved, because it is that on account of which all others exist. Its permanence is ensured by the divinity of its Head as co-equal and co-eternal with the Father and the Holy Spirit. The Church has ever been, and will ever be, triumphant throughout all time.

Membership privileges and responsibility

The necessary qualifications for membership of the Church were repentance of former sins and submission to baptism in the name of Jesus Christ (Acts 2:33) which carried with it the demand of faith in Jesus Christ as God and Saviour.

The privileges of membership acquired at baptism were:

1. The Christian became reconciled with God through appropriating to himself Christ's satisfaction for sin (Romans 5:10; 6:4–7; Colossians 1:21–22). His past life of sin no longer stood against him in his account with God. He was justified.
2. He was sanctified, and henceforth was called 'holy', because he belonged to God by the consecration of baptism (1 Corinthians 6:11).
3. He received the gift of the Holy Spirit (Acts 2:38) as a supernatural power within him.
4. He was admitted to the common life and sacraments of the Christian brotherhood.

Responsibility: on his part, he was bound, so far as he could, to live up to the high standard of that life, 'to put on the new man, which after God hath been created in righteousness and holiness of truth' (Ephesians 4:24).

The new life, to which the convert was introduced by his baptism, was the practical expression of the relation in which he stood to God as a member of His people. His life was henceforth given up to the service of God. And that service was the worship of God in the public gatherings of worship and in the holiness of his private life. By baptism the Christian died to the world, and so the negative, prohibitive, sphere of the law had no longer any meaning for him (Romans 6:3; Colossians 3:5–12). His life was consecrated to Christ (Romans 12:1–2), who is its goal (Romans 14:8), its example (Philippians 2:5; 1 Peter 2:21–24), and the source of its spiritual strength (2 Corinthians 12:9; Ephesians 4:16). His body is the sacred temple of the Holy Spirit (1 Corinthians 6:19), a member of Christ, and therefore personal holiness and purity are his natural condition. The Christian must be ever on his guard, watchful and vigilant, fasting, ever in arms against temptation (1 Thessalonians 5:8; Ephesians 6:10–17), and praying without ceasing (1 Thessalonians 5:17). His mind is set on things above, not on things that are upon the earth (Colossians 3:2). But as he is on the earth he has to perform his human duties and to bring into all his relations with fellow-men principles in accord with this high and ideal life.

The duty of the Church

The Church has constantly to prove herself. Even when she is in full possession of His promise, she can fall away from God. The visible Church of God is not the same as the community of the elect in the consummated Kingdom of God. The visible Church is still under God's judgement. She is therefore exhorted, on her journey towards the peace of her Sabbath, to lift 'drooping hands and weak knees' (Hebrews 12:12); as 'aliens and exiles, to abstain from the passion of the flesh' (1 Peter 2:11); to avoid loving the transient world and its lust, and to do the will of God (1 John 2:15–17);

to repent once again of evil works (Revelation 2:5), and to 'contend' against the demonic powers of this world (Ephesians 6:12).

Finally, the Church is delegated to zealously guard and faithfully transmit the word of God. Faithfully to maintain God's message of salvation, personally to live upon it, and ministerially to preach it throughout the world, is the appointed office of the Church; the instrument of her conflict and the crown of her glory,

The way of the Church is not easy, but its struggles and its tribulations, its persistence and its trust can all be seen in the context of God's promise of certain victory. By the power of the risen Lord, she is given strength to overcome patiently and lovingly the afflictions and hardships which assail her from within and without, and to show forth in the world the mystery of the Lord until at last it will be revealed in total splendour.

> Crowns and thrones may perish,
> Kingdoms rise and wane;
> But the church of Jesus
> Constant will remain:
> Gates of hell can never
> 'Gainst that church prevail;
> We have Christ's own promise —
> And that cannot fail.
>
> (Sabine Baring-Gould)

SKIN DEEP CHRISTIANITY

Reverend Ian Sweeney

Reverend Ian Sweeney was born on 4 July 1965. He is the pastor of two Seventh-day Adventist Churches in Sheffield. He has been engaged in pastoral work in Sheffield since 1991. Formerly, his ministry was conducted in the Moss Side area of Manchester. Ian is married to Jennifer and they celebrated their tenth wedding anniversary in August 1997. They have three children: two boys and one girl.

KEY SCRIPTURE: GALATIANS 3:26–28

I cannot speak for anyone else, but I was hooked by the year-long trial of O. J. Simpson. The various twists and turns of the case were constantly being analysed and evaluated in my mind. Often times I role-played the events in courtroom number 103 in Los Angeles. Never mind that Judge Ito was presiding over the case, I became a judge too. Never mind that Marcia Clark was the chief prosecutor, I was prosecuting too. Never mind that Johnny Cochrane was part of the defence dream team, I also was there preaching, in my summing up, and crying out 'if the hat doesn't fit, you gotta acquit'. I don't know about you, but I was gripped.

On Tuesday 10.00 a.m. Pacific Time, the United States practically came to a standstill to await the verdict. Even at the White House, all presidential briefings were postponed as the President followed the proceedings. The tension was unbearable, as Judge Ito went through the various preliminaries prior to the reading of the jury's verdict. My heart was in my mouth.

While watching the programme *Court TV* last night, it was

39

said that on hearing the verdict 'not guilty', black Americans on the whole rejoiced, whilst white Americans were dismayed. Robert Shapiro said that Johnny Cochrane had dealt the race card from the bottom of the pack. One juror is alleged to have told her daughter that although she believed O. J. was guilty of the crime, the lying testimony of the clearly racist ex-policeman, Mark Fuhrmann, undermined the prosecution's case. The Los Angeles police department had braced themselves for a violent whiplash from black and ethnic minority communities in Los Angeles in case the jury returned a 'guilty' verdict. In following this case it seems to me that for many Americans, the innocence or guilt of O. J. Simpson had no deeper basis than the colour of his skin. For many, the issue of his innocence or guilt was only 'skin deep'.

Skin deep Christianity in church

Experience has shown me that, for many Christians, evaluations are made of one another, not on the commonality and unity of being washed in the blood of Jesus Christ, but rather on the colour of our skin. In July 1997 in Sheffield, the Churches ran a tent crusade. I was the evangelist and my name and number was advertised as the person to contact for further information. Very early one morning I received a call from a lady who gave her name and said that she was the leader of a small group of house Christians, who met in the north of the City of Sheffield. She expressed a desire to come but there were a few doubts in her mind, and so she enquired if her group would be welcomed. I said 'of course!' She asked about a few of our beliefs and she was happy with the responses. Then she asked the question 'if we come, will we be swamped by a lot of black people?' When the telephone suddenly wakes me up from my sleep, I do not generally think at my best, and I can say things which I later regret. But the Lord Jesus issued a command to my tongue, 'peace be still'. I said nothing. The silence was embarrassing. I think she understood the silent rebuke, because after a few minutes, she began to stammer and stumble with her words and she concluded the conversation by saying 'we'll need to pray about it'. I said 'please do'. She never turned up, but if she had, Lord knows that I, who rarely greet with a hug and a holy kiss, would have given her one. What hindered her from Christian fellowship with Seventh-day Adventists had nothing to do with bad publicity concerning Waco, or theological difference. Her hindrance was the evaluation of fellow Christians that only went skin deep.

Racism and prejudice have, unfortunately, been a part of the very fabric of the Christian Church from its inception. The racism of the early Christian Church was not the result of God's design but of man's sinfulness. Of the apostle Peter, we through the gospel are made well aware that he was impulsive and violent (John 18:10), and possessed a filthy tongue with which he could curse with the worst of men (Matthew 26:74). And then, Acts 10 reveals another flaw in Peter's character. To put it bluntly, he was a racist. Many of us are familiar with the story of God's response to Peter's prejudice and racism. A vision was given showing a sheet with all manner of unclean animals of which Peter, a God-fearing Jew, was told to eat. He was puzzled as to why God should command him to eat of those unclean animals. Acts 10:19, 20 (NIV) reads: 'While Peter was still thinking about the vision, the Spirit said to him, "Simon, three men are looking for you. So get up and go downstairs. Do not hesitate to go with them, for I have sent them."' The three men who were looking for Peter came from Cornelius' house, a Gentile centurion living in Caearea. Now Peter seems to have understood why God gave him a vision, for on reaching Cornelius' home he tells his host: 'You are well aware that it is against our law for a Jew to associate with a Gentile or visit him. But God has shown me that I should not call any man impure or unclean. So when I was sent for, I came without raising any objection . . . ' (verses 28, 29).

The Christian author Ellen White makes the comment: 'How carefully the Lord worked to overcome the prejudice against the Gentiles that had been so firmly fixed in Peter's mind by his Jewish training!' (*Acts of the Apostles* (Pacific Press, Ontario, Canada, 1911), p. 136).

Peter seemed to have struggled to overcome his racism and prejudice to the point that, some time later, Paul publicly condemned him for his attitude. You can read of this in Galatians 2:11–14.

There is a saying, 'what goes around, comes around'. The Christian Church is still wrestling with issues of prejudice and racism. In the six years that I spent as a student, it was often proudly announced that Newbold College is a mini United Nations. We had up to 41 nationalities living in peace and harmony. Be that as it may, my friends, the Seventh-day Adventist faces an ongoing challenge of countering what I term 'Skin Deep Christianity'. The Church is not afraid to challenge theological differences and diversities, but of RACISM, PREJUDICE, TRIBALISM, NATIONALISM, CASTE SYSTEMS, APARTHEID and the like, we can be deafly silent.

Learn the lesson

One of the greatest lessons that I learned during my time as a student was not in the classroom. I'm still trying to get my head around some of those deep theological concepts taught by Doctor Metzing in the class. One of the great lessons I learned was that God's family was not to be divided by race, language, tribe or culture, but rather God's family embraces every race, language, tribe and culture, and that I can experience a unity with my brothers and sisters through the blood of Jesus Christ. My evaluation of others ought not to be skin deep, so that I can love others from my heart. I am still learning that the things which separate us are not as important as the Spirit of God that unites us. I can't change my colour: I was born black and will die black. What God has made me, I am happy and proud of. I cannot change my culture. I am very much bound by it and live through it. My culture largely determines how I worship, how I preach, and how I praise God. It is not the differences of race or culture in the family of God that are supremely important. What is supremely important in the family of God, is the ONENESS, which implies that my skin colour is not better, it is just different. My culture is not better, it is just different. And though we are different, because of Jesus, we are one family. We must learn to live and appreciate our differences in Christ.

Conclusion

In closing, permit me to paraphrase the words of the apostle Paul to the Galatians in chapter 3, verses 26–28, changing the second person plural 'you' to the first person plural 'we':

> We are all sons and daughters of God through faith in Christ Jesus, for all of us who were baptized into Christ have clothed ourselves with Christ. There is neither Jew nor Greek, slave nor free, male nor female, [Hutu nor Tutsi, Croatian nor Serbian nor Bosnian, Conservative nor Labour, North nor South, East nor West, small Island nor big Island, Brahmin nor untouchable, postgraduate nor undergraduate, lecturer nor student, rich nor poor, Loyalist nor Republican, black nor white] for we are all ONE in Christ Jesus.

OUR APPROACH TO GOD IN PRAYER

Reverend Vicky Merriman-Johnson

Reverend Vicky Merriman-Johnson hails from Nigeria, and is a minister at Manor Methodist Church in the London Mission, South Bermondsey, south-east London. She studied at the Centre for Black and White Christian Partnership in Birmingham between 1987 and 1989, on the Certificate of Theology course. She has a BA and MA in Race and Ethnic Studies. Her real focus in ministry is working with young people: encouraging and listening to them, and enabling them to reach their full potential through activities such as conferences and seminars regarding black issues, music in worship, as well as giving assistance with career prospects. Vicky has established a Supplementary School, in which she is a key person in ensuring its development.

KEY SCRIPTURE: MARK 10:21

Jesus, looking at him, loved him and said, 'you lack one thing; go, sell what you own and give the money to the poor, and you will have treasure in heaven; then come follow me'.

Aim: to examine our intentions and inward expectations when we approach God in prayer.

Introduction: have you ever asked God a question, and all the time you were asking you had already made up your mind regarding the answer you would accept, and what answer you were not prepared to accept? Have you ever prayed like that? I know I have!

This rich young man in Mark's Gospel ran up to Jesus and

knelt before him and asked a question. Three things are outstanding about the man's action towards Jesus.

1. *He knew how to approach Jesus* — he ran! Others might approach Jesus tentatively or cautiously, but not this man — he ran. Lucy Campbell, an African-American songwriter, sang in one of her songs: 'If you have a problem take up your cross and run to Jesus.' This man not only ran, he knelt, 50 years before Paul's inspiring letter to the Philippians: 'at the name of Jesus every knee shall bow' (Philippians 2:9–11). Edward Perronet wrote this hymn: 'All hail the power of Jesus' name, let angels prostrate fall. O that with yonder sacred throng we at his feet may fall.' This man knew how to approach Jesus, the King of kings, and the Lord of lords.

2. *He knew how to address Jesus* — he said 'good Teacher'. He addressed Jesus with respect and gave him the honour due. The Greek word used here is *agathos* which the Old Testament used for God in Psalm 100: 'for the Lord is good'. Jesus said to him 'why do you call me good, only God is good'. We probably read our Lord's response as a rebuke, but a closer look might suggest that it could be astonishment on Jesus' part, rather than admonishment. Could it be that Jesus is surprised that this rich young man had an insight comparable to Peter and Martha, who declared 'You are the Christ'?

3. *He knew whom to ask* — some of us have important questions, but we go around asking the wrong people. This man knew whom to ask! When you have a problem Jesus has got the answer. He not only has the answer but He is the answer, for he said 'I am the Way, the Truth, and the Life . . . '. John the Baptist had a question, so he sent his disciples to Jesus. Nicodemus had a question and late at night he came to ask Jesus. This rich young man knew who to pose the question to for an answer.

But! You could hear this 'but' coming, couldn't you? There was one thing disturbing about this man. He was rich, and he had so much to lose. How much like this man are some of us? I look at this section of the story and say to myself, well, I'm not rich, I don't have a lot of money, I don't own my own house or any other possession to write home about. After all, Jesus was talking to a 'man' not a 'woman'. Some of us might say we don't even own a car, we are still playing the lottery waiting for the stroke of luck, and therefore this passage can't be addressing us!

Well, God showed me that it wasn't riches in wealth he was referring to, but being in a right relationship with Him. Jesus said if your right hand gets in the way of serving Him, cut it off. So Jesus told this man to go sell his goods, which was the obstruction to a right relationship with God.

This rich young man on the outside was a picture of perfection, a paradigm of preparedness, he was correct and proper in his etiquette; after all he was a Pharisee. But stop to take a closer look at his inward expectation. He approached Jesus in the correct way and asked his question, but he already made up his mind regarding the answer he would accept. His expectation is a bit out of kilter with Kingdom ethics.

I go back to the question I posed at the beginning: 'have you ever prayed and asked God for something and all the while you already made up your mind regarding the answer you would accept?' Have you?

That is *pretentious* praying. You are pretending you really want to hear what God is saying, unless God says what it is you want to hear. You are just asking God to ratify the motion, or is it emotion? You are praying from the head and not the heart. You say the 23rd Psalm 'The Lord is my Shepherd, *I see what I want*'. You ask God to bless the decision you already made, instead of saying 'your will be done, Lord'.

It is *presumptuous* praying because you are presuming to know more than God, anticipating God. After all, you know what you need! A few years ago I wanted to buy my own house and I kept saying to the Lord 'God I want a mortgage', over and over again, without asking God what he really wants for me.

It is *preposterous* praying. If you think you know more than God, that's preposterous. God answered Job's questioning with the words: 'who are you to question my wisdom with your ignorant empty words! Were you there when I laid the foundations of the earth?' (Job 38:4). Deutero-Isaiah says 'Neither are your ways, my ways' (Isaiah 55:8). The Psalmist says 'The Lord rules over all the nations; his glory is above the heavens' (Psalm 148:13).

The young man was an achiever, he was a Pharisee — he kept the laws. He said to Jesus 'I have observed all the Mosaic Laws'. He was a rich young man. A proper and upright-standing member of the community, he therefore thought the way to the Kingdom was through achieving: 'what must I do to receive eternal life?' He did not know that it was through God's Grace that we enter the Kingdom.

Jesus looked at him with love and told him to sell everything and come follow Him. Because Jesus loved him, he knew what he needed and what was best for him. Our heavenly Father knows what we need and what's best for us.

Jesus said to the young man, you need just one more thing — *a radical trust in me.* You need to trust me and trust what I tell you to do. When you have prayed, you need to trust God to do what's best for you in that situation. Jesus was saying to the man 'you need me as the centre of your life'. Right now, money and possessions may be the centre of your life. What is at the centre of your life? Jesus is saying we need to rely on Him to supply all our needs, to trust him when we can't see him, trust him when we don't know why. Trust him when the storms of life are raging and the clouds are dark and hanging low, trusting him when nothing is going right; trust him who knows what is best for us. The Lord ever loves and cares for His own. The Good Shepherd knows what's best for us.

'I am trusting thee, Lord Jesus, trusting only thee, trusting thee for full salvation; great and free' (Frances Ridley Havergal).

FROM FEAR TO FORGIVENESS

Reverend Inderjit Bhogal

Reverend Inderjit Bhogal is a Christian with roots in the Sikh faith. He is a Methodist minister and is currently Director of the Urban Theology Unit in Sheffield. He has developed a wide circuit experience through working in Wolverhampton and Sheffield.

Inderjit is committed to the promotion and achievement of racial justice, the development of inter-faith relationships, adult theological education, and social and economic justice for all.

KEY SCRIPTURE: JOHN 20:19

. . . the doors of the house where the disciples had met were locked for fear of the Jews. Jesus came and stood among them and said: 'Peace be with you.'

What a picture of Christian discipleship! These followers of Jesus have just had up to three years of training with Him. They have had personal tuition with Him. They have debated theology, explored the Scriptures, puzzled, prayed, worshipped together. They have even been on placements — for practical experience – in twos in their case. At the end of it they are a bag of nerves! A terrified bunch. And then they are ordained.

Does this sound familiar? If after three years of training you feel like this, you should not be surprised. But Jesus commissions His disciples: 'As the father sent me, so I send you.' He breathes His Spirit into them and sends then out with just one piece of advice or wisdom: 'Be forgiving.'

48

The text begins with fear and moves on to forgiveness. The spirit of forgiveness sets people free from fears — and helps them to move on in discipleship. If fear can paralyse discipleship, forgiveness can free it.

There is a widespread habit of regarding the Gospel according to John as the 'Spiritual Gospel'. But its spirituality is not always seen as arising from real-life situations.

Recent scholarship (e.g. *Johannine Faith and Liberating Community* by David Rensberger and *Becoming the Children of God* by Wes Howard-Brooke) has paid greater attention to the social and historical setting out of which this gospel emerged, and to the fears and conflicts in which the Johannine community was involved. And one of the suggestions today is that John's Christian community was quite small, almost sectarian, and founded on a strong and public confession of faith in Jesus. John's community lived out their faith in circumstances of open persecution of Christians by the predominant Jewish community. Some chose to be secret disciples, like Nicodemus. But those who tried to engage with the neighbouring community faced persecution . . . they were an easy target. People could join them by publicly professing faith in Jesus, as seen in the story of Nicodemus and the man born blind whose sight was restored.

What kept this little community going was regular worship, meeting with each other, holding on to each other – often meeting behind locked doors. So the reflections we term John's gospel emerge out of a situation of crisis, conflict and open hostility between Christian and Jews. The Jews come to represent the hostile world out there, indeed anyone that is not 'one of us'.

It needs to be stated before we go any further that Churches need to confess in penitence and shame that John's Gospel has not been good for Jewish–Christian relationships over the last two centuries. We need to do this again and again, and to seek forgiveness from Jewish sisters and brothers.

John's gospel gives hints also of conflict within and between Christian communities — as seen, for example, in tensions between those who have 'seen the Lord' and those who have not (John 20:24f.). John's Jesus prays that 'they may be one'. It is this community with all its internal struggles and fears of the world out there; it is this fragile, fearful people who are commissioned for mission and for ministry. They are the ones who are to continue Jesus' ministry of sharing in God's mission. 'As the father sent me, so I send you.' The Johannine Jesus Christ makes no distinction between his ministry and the ministry of his community. They are part of the ministry of Christ.

The more I read this gospel story, the more I see so much of the contemporary Church, discipleship and world in it. Small congregations feel vulnerable, often fearful of the world out there.

I share in the ministry of Christ with a small Christian community at Wincobank in Sheffield. The Wincobank Estate was designated in the 1920s and is referred to as the Flower Estate. All the streets are named after flowers. The estate is no garden city now. It is run down. Many of the houses are boarded up, because people refuse to move into the area. Some residents have placed iron grids outside their windows to prevent break-ins.

Our little Christian community gives priority to working with the children of the estate. We meet in a tiny, dilapidated chapel; our windows get broken regularly. We have a wonderful time in worship, which is our main activity. We gather from 10.00 a.m. on a Sunday morning. Children lead the first half-hour of worship then they continue their activity in a Sunday Club. When the preacher for the day eventually gets a look in — she or he is encouraged to lead a bible-study style of reflection. We often sit huddled together. Sometimes windows are broken while we worship.

When we were recently reflecting on our text, John 20:19f., I'd only read the words: ' . . . the doors of the house where the disciples had met were locked for fear of the Jews', when Sandra, who is 80 and lives alone, interjected: 'That's like here. People lock their doors for fear.' I know Sandra keeps her doors locked. 'What is your greatest fear, Sandra?' I asked. 'Being broken into by criminals', she said, and added

'It wasn't like this in years gone past'. I asked 'Sandra, what needs to happen *now* in order that you may experience a sense of security again?' She replied 'People need to be given employment so that they have a living and break out of crime'. These words of Sandra's in effect are a summary of nearly 300 pages of the Churches' Report *Unemployment and the Future of Work*.

The disciples of Jesus met behind locked doors — with all their fears. Their fears had certainly drained them of energy. Fear exhausts. They are almost lifeless. Their fears bring them together. They hold on to each other.

We all have our fears, like them, like Sandra. Fears that drain life out of us. Fears that threaten to paralyse us. And what do you do with your fears? How do you move on in discipleship? What resources are there among us, and in the gospel to deal with our fears? Many of our fears are related to others, often people close to us, often people among whom we have to minister.

Fear of Jews remains to this day for so many. Anti-Semitism shows no sign of disappearing. Jews continue to face danger. Synagogues are targets of attack to the extent they have to install security cameras and fencing for protection. And, as I have said, we have to recognize that views like those of John have contributed to this.

Many Christians generally fear people of other faiths. Far from seeing religious diversity as 'within the will and gracious purposes of God' (BCC), it is seen as a threat. Far from seeing Buddhist, Hindu, Islamic, Jewish, Sikh and other cultures as an enrichment of our life, they are seen in terms of loss. When I take my children to school we have to cross a busy road at a pelican crossing. As we wait for the green figure, twenty or so others congregate. And I can see the composition of our neighbourhood: people of different coloured skins and different cultures. It is a delight to see them. I think to myself — this is a sign and a vision of the Kingdom of God. But people in cars and buses passing by, usually at a crawling pace at that time, look out of their windows at us – most of them look in despair at what they see. I can almost

51

hear some of them saying 'I used to live in this area — it's gone downhill'. Some of us rejoice that God has created diversity and difference. We celebrate them. Others despair at it. Many fear those who are different from them — a fear that does not bode well for good relationships. There are white people who fear black people. Politicians build on this fear to tighten up immigration and asylum laws. There are 400 racial attacks a day in Britain. And, of course, there are black people who fear white people. Many small congregations courageously exercise discipleship in hostile environments.

Some versions of our text read that the disciples were meeting behind locked doors 'for fear of the Jewish *authorities*'. Perhaps there is a more accurate translation. Their fears related to those who exercised some control and authority and power over them. We all know such fears. With all our fears, we have to remember that it is people with fears that Jesus commissions. He speaks words of peace and re-assurance to them. He breathes His Spirit into them. And He challenges them. The breath of God is the source of human life in Genesis.

The disciples require new life to be breathed into them — so drained of life they are. Jesus is the one who is crucified. The disciples are the ones from whom life seems to have dissipated: paralysed by fear, unable to handle the world around them. Jesus is risen, and they are the ones he has to bring back to life first. At least they had stuck together and that had sustained them. What bit of strength they had came from a sense of being part of a community.

One function of worship, where people meet together with Jesus in their midst, is to give life and to nourish and to sustain them for mission and ministry. And Jesus gave His disciples one piece of advice: 'be forgiving'. The cycle of this text goes from fear to forgiveness. Forgiveness is about an attitude of graciousness, friendship, penitence, hospitality, and respect — an accommodating, embracing spirit.

We have seen some remarkable symbols of such forgiveness that can restore relationships, reconcile and heal relationships. Nelson Mandela came to Britain with a remarkable spirit of forgiveness when he may have been expected to come with a scolding spirit. Gordon Wilson spoke words of forgiveness to those who took the life of his daughter. Jesuit priests in El Salvador are offering forgiveness to soldiers who murdered their colleagues at the University of Central America. And sometimes forgiveness is not even accepted. Sometimes people fail to see the *need* for forgiveness and like Jesus we may be left praying to God 'Father forgive them . . .'.

From your experience in ministry already, and all of us from our experience of home life, work community or church will be aware that relations are fragile. Individuals and communities demonize each other. Relationships are fragile and flounder. We live in, and exercise Christian discipleship in a broken, divided world in which one of the basic human rights is the freedom from fear. Locking up of doors of homes, of churches, is a salient factor of contemporary life. Ministry is, in so many ways, about helping people work through their fears and hatreds, and to facilitate the process of forgiveness. Forgiveness — the way to it, the way to offer and to receive it, is perhaps a particular ministry of the Church today.

If there is one supreme quality that is desirable and necessary in someone who has pastoral charge in the Church, it is the capacity to forgive, and to facilitate forgiveness.

This is Jesus' chief requirement of those whom *He* commissions to share in His ministry.

THE POWER OF THE CROSS

Bishop Ceebert T. Richards

Bishop Ceebert Richards is the National Overseer of the Church of Jesus Christ Apostolic, England. He is also the pastor of the local church in Sheffield, where he currently resides. He has received a Certificate in Theology, and is a Doctor in Divinity. He is a counsellor and works closely with the Education and Social Services Departments in Sheffield. He is also a Welfare Officer for some schools and counsels disruptive pupils.

> KEY SCRIPTURES: 1 CORINTHIANS 1:17–18;
> GALATIANS 6:14; ISAIAH 52:13; 53:12;
> PHILIPPIANS 2:5–11; 3:20–21

The cross of Christ stands at the heart of our Christian faith. Without it we have no faith, and apart from the truth of it, Christianity becomes only another philosophy of life: a matter of words and ideas. Jesus did not come to give us another set of ideas about God; rather, He came to die for us. Mark 8:31 says 'And he began to teach them, that the Son of man must suffer many things, and be rejected of the elders, and of the chief priests, and scribes, and be killed, and after three days rise again'.

The idea of the cross was integral, as far as Jesus was concerned, to the training of His disciples. He used the reality of the cross to emphasize the need for absolute commitment to the Kingdom. Jesus already knew within Himself what it meant to 'take up the cross'. He wanted us, His followers, to take up our cross and follow Him. In Luke 9:23, Jesus tells us 'if any man will come after me, let him deny himself, and take up his cross daily, and follow me'.

Let us take into consideration the agony that Jesus underwent on the cross for our redemption. As we try to understand the suffering, we will see that there is no virtue in highlighting the pain and horror of the cross for its own sake. We need to enter into the reality of Christ's suffering to some degree, if we are ever to appreciate, firstly, what it means for God to save us through the cross and, secondly, what God has accomplished for everyone of us in the death of Jesus Christ.

Many of us have lived for so long with a domesticated idea of the cross. We have refined it of its horror and in doing that we have robbed it of its power. The Holy Spirit wants us to know the importance of Christ's sacrifice, because the work of the cross should be central to our lives and ministry. The scriptures hide nothing of the shame and agony that was involved for God's beloved Son. It is not simply the fact that he died that is important, it is how he died that has the greatest significance for every one of us.

The Old Testament prophecies concerning the death of Christ place emphasis on the details of his suffering. Isaiah 50:6: 'I gave my back to the smiters, and my cheeks to them that plucked off the hair: I hid not my face from shame and spitting.'

Psalms 22:12–18:

Many bulls have compassed me: strong bulls of Bashan have beset me round. They gaped upon me with their mouths, as a ravening and a roaring lion. I am poured out like water, and all my bones are out of joint: my heart is like wax; it is melted in the midst of my breast. My strength is dried up like a potsherd; and my tongue cleaveth to my jaws; and thou hast brought me into the dust of death. For dogs have compassed me; the assembly of the wicked have enclosed me: they pierced my hands and my feet. I may tell all my bones: they look and stare upon me. They part my garments among them, and cast lots upon my vesture.

In the Church at large, we have brought Jesus down to our

size and we have diminished His death to dimensions that we can handle spiritually, emotionally, and theologically. If we felt the deep horror of the cross, we would know the full extent of our sins and this is what we recoil from within the deeper recesses of our hearts and minds. What happened that day at Calvary was not very pretty. There was no sentiment in a Roman scourging, and Roman crucifixion has been universally recognized as being the cruellest of public execution ever devised. It was a horrific, slow, painful and humiliating death. We need to see the depth of Calvary, we need to see that everything we can have or be flows from this act of love. Most of all we need to recognize that if we are to live for God, then we need to walk the same way ourselves.

Jesus did not undergo a normal, routine crucifixion, but was subject to the public humiliation of a mock trial before Pontius Pilate during which he was abused, beaten and disfigured. His beard was torn out and a crown of thorns was placed on His head as a gesture of mockery to His claim to be king. In the garden of Gethsemane, He had to face the awful truth that this cup was His and it could be drunk by no one else. The pressure within Him was so intense that He bled from His brow. When the soldiers came to Jesus on the cross they saw that he was dead already, so they did not break His legs. Instead, they pierced His side and blood and water gushed out. This means that Jesus had quite literally died of a broken heart. His heart had burst and the blood had congealed. The blood and plasma had become separated and when He was pierced, they flowed out from His side.

We cannot begin to speak of His spiritual sufferings. These things are hidden from us because there is no way that we could comprehend what it meant for Jesus to be forsaken by His Father. The cry that soared from His lips, which echoed the words of Psalms 22:1: 'My God, my God, why hast Thou forsaken me? Why art Thou so far from helping me, and from the words of my roaring?' — these words contain depths of suffering that we will never be able to understand. We must see that none of these events were by chance. Man took Him to the cross, but was not in charge of the proceedings that day! This is the awesome truth of Calvary. God was in control. God was offering up His only-begotten Son for the souls of men. We recoil from the facts, because it only serves to underline even more clearly the extent of our guilt.

Acts 2:23 reads: 'Him, being delivered by the determinate counsel and foreknowledge of God, ye have taken, and by wicked hands have crucified and slain.' God in some mysterious way laid our guilt upon Jesus and through His suffering we were set free. Isaiah 53:4–5 declares 'Surely He hath borne our griefs and carried our sorrows: yet we did esteem Him stricken, smitten of God and afflicted. But He was wounded for our transgressions, he was bruised for our iniquities, the chastisement of our peace was upon Him; and with His stripes we are healed.'

The power of the cross for us lies in the fact that every detail of the experience of Jesus in His suffering has dynamic significance for us at every point of our need. Ever since the fall of man, Satan has kept men and women under oppression. They have been bound in chains of sin, sickness, depression and despair, which has been the hallmark of human experience. Man has become subject to every kind of suffering and affliction as a result of his disobedience to God.

On the cross, every spiritual and emotional bondage, every affliction which Satan has brought to man, through man's disobedience, has been reversed in the power of the cross at Calvary. The power of the cross lies in the fact that Jesus Christ took all these elements unto Himself on the cross and broke their power. He overcame every negative factor that has ever threatened man, and He broke the power of Satan who masterminded all these forces to bring man to destruction.

It is not enough to wonder at the work of Jesus on the cross. However, for that work to be effective in us we need to receive it into our own lives. It was in the power of the Holy Spirit that Jesus offered Himself for us, 'How much more shall the blood of Christ, who through the eternal Spirit offered himself without spot to God, purge your conscience from dead works to serve the living God?' (Hebrews 9:14).

It is as we allow the Holy Spirit to do the same work of overcoming sin, the affliction and the power of death in us, that we will enter into the true victory of Calvary.

God bless you all. Amen.

THE DESIRED TRINITY

The Most Reverend Prophetess
Fidelia N. Onyuku-Opukiri (Archbishop)

The Most Reverend Prophetess Fidelia Onyuku-Opukiri (Archbishop) is a native of Odoni in Ijaw in Rivers State, Nigeria. Fidelia came to the United Kingdom in 1966, to join her husband. She has five children: four girls and one boy. She embarked on a programme of studies in pharmacology at the University of London, but her aim was overtaken by her vocation to serve God.

She served in the Cherubim and Seraphim Church, Tottenham from 1973 to 1978. She is the founder of the Born Again Christ Healing Church, which was first established in London in 1979. In 1990 she received her Certificate in Theology from the University of Birmingham. For many years Fidelia served a number of different organizations. For example, from 1985 to 1987, she was the Vice-Chair of the Council of African and Afro-Caribbean Churches (UK). She also served on the Executive Board of the Free Churches Women's Council from 1989 to 1993.

She is a member of the Editorial Board for *Church and Race* magazine, produced by the Churches Commission for Racial Justice. She is also a member of the Management Committee of the African Churches Council for Immigration and Social Justice (ACCIS), and an executive committee member of the Centre for Black and White Christian Partnership.

KEY SCRIPTURE: JOHN 15:1–7

In the first verse of this portion, Jesus speaks in His usual poetic manner, though in parable. He proclaims 'I am the

59

true vine, and my Father is the husbandman'. Looking into this statement, prayerfully and meditatively, the Holy Spirit reveals the truth of God's nature, will and desire to all mankind.

Jesus says He is 'the true vine'. The key words here are 'TRUE' and 'VINE'. 'TRUE' meaning 'real, faithful, loyal, lawful, reliable' etc. 'VINE' – a fruit-bearing plant — e.g. the grapevine.

It is obvious that Jesus is not literally a plant or a tree for that matter. So what is Jesus saying? What does the scripture say He is? He is the son of God, the Saviour and Redeemer. Jesus Himself says in John 14:9–10 'He that hath seen me hath seen the Father . . . I am in the Father and the Father in me.' The Holy Spirit and the scripture therefore confirm that Jesus is the Son of God as well as God, He is the Saviour and Redeemer of all mankind. The emphasis on His statement is that whatever Jesus is, He is the only real, genuine lawful and faithful of His kind, no one can be compared to Him. Therefore, of all different gods worshipped by different nations of the world, Jesus is the only genuine God.

Now we ask 'why did Jesus have to use the vine in this parable?' After all, there are many other trees which in human eyes would be considered much greater. With a little con-sideration, the speciality in the vine tree is revealed: sweet, nourishing, fruit-bearing plant, e.g. grapevine. The sweet and nourishing fruit, which maintains health, therefore is able to give life. To go even deeper, when this fruit is fermented it produces alcohol, which when taken is intoxicating and can change human behaviour.

In other words, Jesus declares that He is the only genuine, sure, faithful, lawful, and reliable living God. 'Living God', because He is alive and able to make things happen, and create changes where it is necessary or where it is required, which is why many of God's people live by faith and experience God's miracle of changes in different situations of life. There is power in the blood of Jesus Christ. Amen.

The second statement says 'My Father is the husband-man'. Here Jesus gives the truth about His Father being the boss, who owns the vine. He is the keeper of the vine. No one else has right to the vine except the Father.

Verse 2 states 'Every branch in me that beareth not fruit he taketh away and every branch that beareth fruit, he purgeth it, that it may bring forth more fruit'. Here we learn that this vine has branches and the branches are expected to bear plenty of fruits. The husbandman is in charge of the branches. He grooms and cares for them, cutting off the branches that do not produce fruit. He does not compromise with or tolerate any type of unproductivity. In other words, God is the boss who cares and comes to the aid of all that believe and trust in him and His only-begotten Son Jesus Christ.

(Note: We skip verse 3 and return to it later.)

Verse 4 says 'Abide in me, and I in you. As the branch cannot bear fruit of itself, except it abide in the vine; no more can you except you abide in me.' As we read this verse the message becomes clearer. Christ urges all believers to abide in Him and He will also abide in us. Just as the branch of the vine cannot live except it is firmly attached to the vine so also we cannot live except we are firmly attached to the vine, i.e. CHRIST.

Verse 5. Here the parable is explained: 'I am the true vine, and you are the branches. He that abideth in me, and I in him, the same bringeth forth much fruit, for without me you can do nothing.' Now we find out that the vine does not only involve Jesus Christ and the Father, it also involves us, the individuals who believe in God and Christ. We are the branches and we are expected to abide in Christ because our lives are meaningless without Him, and we are incapable of bearing fruits without the nourishing sap that the vine draws via its roots to the branches.

So far there are two words that keep repeating themselves: 'abide' and 'fruits'.

How do we abide in Christ? Or, what does it mean to abide? It is good to see the well-bonded relationship between the vine and the branches. Believe in Christ the Son of God and the Father in totality. Not wavering, not doubting and opposing the word of God. Pray always, read the word of God constantly. Be a member of a lively Church where Christ and the Gospel are alive and the Holy Spirit works in visions, revelations and prophecies. So there will be no assumption of righteousness. God, Christ and the Holy Spirit are the leaders and directors of our lives. We will be scolded and chastised when we do wrong, forgiven and healed when we repent. We must take part in all Church activities, be it bible studies, prayer fellowship, church services, meetings, all-night vigils, etc. We must pay our dues in the Church (i.e. tithes, offerings, alms-giving, etc.). Christians who separate their money from worshipping God have totally lost the way. They should go into the scriptures for the truth: Malachi 3:8–10; Haggai 1:1–11; Leviticus 23:1–22 and 37; Acts 4:33–37, 5:1–11, and many others. You cannot claim any blessing from God if you are a mean person.

The Church of God in general must also abide in Christ by keeping and teaching the truth as given in the holy scriptures: not wavering, not compromising. Avoid teachers and ministers who deny the Virgin Birth and the Resurrection of Jesus Christ, which constitute the foundation of our Christian belief. This is anti-Christ. We must avoid opposition of scriptural teachings, stop encouraging sins and the lusts of flesh such as adultery, fornication, homosexuality, lesbianism, abortion and many other things on which the scriptures have given specific teachings but we, because of our own wickedness, would like to change to suit our lives and requirements. We must understand that the commandments of God are not for us to toss about as we please. The rules are laid down for us to follow, and we are expected to resist the temptation to fall. Our personal wisdom, opinion, knowledge and understanding do not change the will and word of God. We shall be judged by every action we take. Saints of God gave their lives to establish these words of God, so we must not make a mockery of the priceless sacrifices of the Saints, as if we are here to undo the work of the Saints and uproot the Church of God. (Hence anti-Christ.)

Verse 3 says 'Now you are clean through the word which I

have spoken unto you'. The early Apostles whom Christ addressed directly when this sermon was preached were just ordinary people with all the sins and faults of ordinary people. It was not until Jesus came and preached His gospel to them that they became aware of their sinful state. They received the salvation of God and their lives and ways changed, so they became clean. Jesus therefore urged them to abide in Him (Jesus Christ) for the maintenance of the salvation they had received. So the word 'Abide' is also an encouragement to continue living in the salvation of God. Of course we are the apostles of today, and God with these same words urges us to continue living in His salvation. It is a very dangerous thing for a Christian to feel that he/she has made it in Christ. That is to say I have known Christ, and relax in prayer, fasting and worshipping God. The minute we relax, the devil views our laxity as loopholes through which he can come into our lives and mess us up. Then we can no longer sing the song of the Saints ('Things I used to do, I do them no more').

The word FRUIT. What does it mean? It is obvious that we as human beings cannot literally produce fruits like the vine. 'Fruits' as the Holy Spirit revealed it to me are in three categories.

The *first one* is the ability to live our daily lives (i.e. have a roof over our heads, have a job to go to and earn our living), thus, the fruit of our hands' work. Every thing we are, own and receive comes from God, hence 'for without me ye can do nothing'.

The *second fruit* is the ability to live a righteous life. Many people will not come to Church because of the guilt of sin, and some are frightened of becoming Christians because of all the so-called 'righteous qualities' that are required of Christians. What they do not know is that no one can achieve righteousness without Christ. The house of God is the only place where we can receive aid (i.e. prayer, the word of God, strength and encouragement), which will lead us to righteousness. Our lives and surroundings are filthy and corrupt, so we cannot achieve righteousness by ourselves.

Righteousness is not man-made, it is the grace of God given through the blood of Jesus Christ. So God calls everyone, however sinful you are, to come and worship Him. By the time you know it, you will find that changes have taken place in your life. Changes you did not plan or expect, but received through the power that is in the blood of Jesus Christ. 'Not by power, not by might but by my spirit, says the Lord.' Hence, the Pentecostals sing the song of testimonies which says:

> Things I used to do, I do them no more
> Things I used to say, I say them no more
> Things I used to do, I do them no more
> There is a great change since I was born.

Chorus: Great change since I was born
> Great change since I was born
> Great change since I was born
> There is a great change since I was born.

The *third fruit* is the ability to overcome spiritual forces. Many people would argue against the existence of such forces, but the scriptures and Jesus Christ say they exist, and many people experience them. They are the culprits of sudden mishaps in our lives. They create barriers and problems against the will of God, which is aimed at doing us good and giving us victory in all of our endeavours. Spiritual forces are satanic, we cannot see them but we feel the pressure they assert on us and our surroundings. They strike when we least expect it and we experience the misfortunes they cause us. Misfortunes such as sudden and untimely death, health deterioration, lack of progress, sins, and many other things which undermine human happiness. God and Christ are the highest spiritual beings. Where Christ rules and the Holy Spirit is alive, whatever havoc is planned by these forces is revealed by the Holy Spirit in visions and prophecies, and remedies are also given to combat the plans of the enemy.

Verse 6 says 'If a man abide not in me, he is cast forth as a branch, and is withered; and men gather them, and cast them into the fire and they are burned'. If we do not abide in Christ, we lose our rights as people created in the image of God. We forfeit our rights to be gods, which we gained from creation when God gave man right of ownership. We hand over our rights to people, creatures, and spiritual forces. This is also the problem of evolution. We become disadvantaged, cheated, our lives endangered and we could even lose our lives, all because we are ignorant of our rights, which are only derived from the knowledge of God. Life becomes meaningless and less progressive, hence the branch is cast forth and men gather them and cast them into the fire and they are burned. Life becomes miserable, painful and short.

Verse 7 says 'If you abide in me and my words abide in you, ye shall ask what ye will and it shall be done unto you'. This is a sure promise that gives me great joy, because I have tasted, trusted and tried it. I confirm that God's promise is true. Abide in Christ and let His word abide in you (i.e. keep the word of God as it is in the scriptures, not wavering, doubting or using your own opinion and wisdom) and ask whatever you will. Worship God according to His will in the scriptures and you will ask whatever you will and it shall be done unto you. There are no limitations to what you can ask as long as it is asked in righteousness and love. God is able and there is power in the blood of Jesus Christ. Amen.

This is the desired TRINITY:

1. *Jesus Christ*, the vine: on whom we the branches depend for our spiritual and physical strength and well-being.
2. *God the Father Almighty*, the husbandman: who owns the vine (Jesus Christ) and the branches (people of God), and takes care of both for our sakes and for His own namesake.
3. *'We' the people of God*, the branches: we the people of God who must abide in the vine (Jesus Christ) so that we will bear fruits for our own sake. While we bear fruits the Father takes care of our lives and our physical and spiritual well-being. This fulfils the saying of Christ which is in John 14:20, 'I am in my Father and you in me, and I in you'.

65

I pray that God gives understanding to all who read or hear these words that they will yield good fruit in us and bring about immeasurable blessings which will lead us all to be part of the desired trinity, IN JESUS' NAME. AMEN.

IS JESUS IN YOUR BOAT?

Reverend Novette Thompson

Reverend Novette Thompson is a Methodist minister serving in London North-West District of the Methodist Church. She is also in pastoral charge of the diverse and multi-ethnic Neasden Methodist Church, which is within the Wembley Circuit. She has been serving in this capacity since 1992, and was ordained in 1993. Novette has interests in many areas of ministry, but in particular, and at the moment, she is involved in womanist and black theology, and pastoral care.

KEY SCRIPTURES: JOHN 6:16–21;
ISAIAH 43:1–3A

When evening came, his disciples went down to the sea, got into a boat and started across the sea to Capernaum. It was now dark, and Jesus had not yet come to them. The sea rose because a strong wind was blowing. When they had rowed about three or four miles, they saw Jesus walking on the sea and drawing near to the boat. They were frightened, but he said to them, 'It is I; do not be afraid.' Then they were glad to take him into the boat and immediately the boat was at the land to which they were going.

(John 6:16–21 RSV)

The sea can be a terrifying place to be. Like so many of the natural forces, we have no control over the waves of the sea. Can you imagine what it would be like to be tossed by those overwhelming waves — waves as big as a multi-storey building? We are powerless against those crashing torrents, great walls of water. Both Paul and the disciples of Jesus found themselves, more than once, in peril on the sea.

Jesus says to the disciples out there on the rough Sea of Galilee ' "It is I, do not be afraid." And they were glad to take him into the boat, and immediately the boat was at the land to which they were going.' John's gospel is full of symbolic meaning, so whenever you read it, don't just take it at face value. John intends for you to search for the deeper, spiritual meaning, which is there in every event he records. John was not just interested in giving a straight biography of Jesus' life, he wanted to show people the *significance* of this man who came into the world. Our text tells us that as soon as Jesus got into the boat, the boat reached the land they had been heading for. One minute they were out on stormy waters, and the next they were safely on land. There's no doubt that the disciples did reach land safely that night, but there's more to the story than that.

The symbol of the boat

One of the early Christian symbols of the Church was a boat with sails. The Church was a boat, violently tossed on the stormy seas of life. The symbol of the boat probably developed as a result of Christians hearing this story being circulated in the churches. There were times when the Church went through very dismal periods. Times of false accusations, such as the incident of the Fire of Rome, when Christians were blamed for starting it. Times when Jesus seemed far from them. When Jesus came into the boat in the story, it was a symbol of the Church suddenly recognizing the presence of Jesus. He was there after all, and their hope was renewed. When Jesus was at the heart of this body of people called Christians, they had passed from death into life. He had stepped into their boat.

Our daily storms

Everyday, somewhere in the world, people battle with tragedy and suffering. The storms of life break hard upon us. Accident, illness, unemployment, unsolicited debt, war and strife. You feel as though you are rowing hard to get to your destination, achieve goals for your life and family; but life seems to batter you. Help may come from friends and family; people may find asylum in another country, but how do we find that inner peace of mind that we need in the midst of the storm? The physical needs may be met, but spiritual resources are also needed to hold on to a deeper sense of calm and assurance.

Have you been through the dark, stormy waters of life? Naturally — from time to time. Can you identify a *moment* when Jesus climbed into your boat, and suddenly there was peace, there was calm, you felt as though you did not have to struggle anymore? Whether as an individual or as the Body of Christ, we need to discern the presence of Jesus particularly when we are facing suffering or tragedy. How will you know that Jesus has climbed into your boat?

His promise

The first thing that should remind you that Jesus has climbed into your boat of suffering or trial, is his *promise* to be with us, 'even to the close of the age' (Matthew 28:20). That was the last promise Jesus made to His disciples before leaving them. He had given them the task of preaching the good news, and He had given them the reassurance that He would be with them. You can know that Jesus is with you, because He has said that he would be.

Even so, in the heat of your trial, it may be difficult to remind yourself of this fact. H. A. Williams uses the illustration of a holiday spent in Marrakesh in Morocco, North Africa, near the Sahara desert. When the wind blows up the desert, the hot sand almost blocks out the sun. You might believe that you don't need to protect yourself from the sun in the usual way, but you would be mistaken. The heat of the sun is just as strong, and you can easily be burnt, regardless of your complexion. It's the same with God. Our problems, like the sand, seem to block God out and we think that He is not there. But God is there, as strong as ever. We just need to believe it.

His sacrifice

We can know that Jesus has climbed into our boat, not just because He said he would, but because He literally did. He stepped into our shoes. He gave up the glory of heaven with God, He became human and stepped into our shoes. He died the death that each one of us should have died. He died in our place, and was raised to life by God the Father. In fact, Jesus was in the boat before we got there. Jesus was tossed on the stormy seas before we got into the boat. Jesus was ahead of us. Any trial of life that you may be going through, Jesus has been there ahead of you.

Conclusion

God, speaking to the people of Israel in exile, says to them 'Fear not, for I have redeemed you. I have called you by name, you are mine. When you pass through the waters, I will be with you; and through the rivers, they shall not overwhelm you; when you walk through fire, you shall not be burned, and the flame shall not consume you' (Isaiah 43:1–2). They were frightened, but He said to them 'It is I; do not be afraid'. Then, they were glad to take him into the boat, and immediately, the boat was at the land to which they were going. Do not be afraid, Jesus is in the boat with you.

Amen.

POWER AND POTENTIAL

Reverend Ronald O. Brown

Reverend Ron Brown was born in Westmoreland, Jamaica and came to the United Kingdom in 1959. He received the Lord Jesus Christ as his personal Saviour on 1 September 1955, and subsequently became a lay preacher and a local Church leader.

He became a member of the New Testament Church of God (NTCG) in 1962, where he served as District Youth Director for a number of years. He was called to full-time ministry in 1963 when he became the pastor for NTCG in Gloucester.

Revd Brown is married to Phyllis and they have two children. Revd Brown and his wife served as missionary overseers of the Church in Ghana from 1982 to 1992. On his return to the United Kingdom, he was appointed as National Overseer for NTCG in 1994. In 1995, the European Bible Seminary awarded him the title of Doctor of Literature. Revd Brown's motto is 'to know Christ better and to make Him better known'.

KEY SCRIPTURE: PSALM 62:11 SAYS:
'POWER BELONGS TO GOD.'

He is the source and origin of all power and His power is available as a source of blessings. He seeks to express and to extend His power through mankind, who is made in His image and likeness. He is the resource and regenerator. Mankind, in co-operation with God and Christ, has the potential to be the expression, the expansion and the extension of God's power.

The Bible says we are His workmanship, which means, we are His finished product, His masterpiece.

On an atomic submarine on the coast of North Africa, the captain, speaking to one of his delegates, said 'We have the capacity to throw the entire continent of Africa off the map'. What power, what potential! What means of utter devastation! It makes the hydrogen bombs dropped on Hiroshima and Nagasaki fade into insignificance. What is man's power? He has learned to co-operate with nature and to turn it to his own destruction, but God's power is for your health, for blessings, for victory, and for sharing Himself with mankind. The sun is the principal source of power for the earth, God is the source of power for the sun, and the source for the universe. Colossians 1:16–17 tells us 'All things were created by Him, and by Him, all things consist'. That means, everything is held together, and is serviced by Him. Our text says 'Power belongs to God'. Jesus says 'All power is given to me in heaven and in earth'. God's power is seen in the creation of this vast universe out of nothing. David says in Psalm 8:3, 4: 'When I consider the heavens, the work of thy fingers, the moon, the stars which thou hast ordained, what is man that thou art mindful of him, or the son of man that thou dost care for him?'

This mass that we call earth, being some 25,000 miles in circumference, is but one of the smaller of God's planets. He is all-powerful, all-knowing, all-seeing and eternal. Job 26:7 says 'He stretches out the north over the empty places and hangs the earth upon nothing'. How could Job know, back in those days, that the earth was hanging suspended upon nothing but the power of God? Job 26:13 continues: 'By his spirit, he garnished the heavens, he formed the crooked serpent.' Isaiah takes up the theme in Isaiah 40:22 and says 'It is he who sits above the circle of the earth'. How could Isaiah know that the earth was round when thousands of years later, scientists were still contending that it was flat?

Isaiah 40:22, 26 continues to say 'He stretches out the heavens like a curtain, and spreads them like a tent to dwell in . . . He who brings out their host by number, calling them

72

all by name; by the greatness of his might, and because he is strong in power, not one is missing.' Not one thing created ever failed, never a cosmic accident, never has one of those planets moved out of its axis, been late or collided, clashing with one another. All are held in place by the hand of this mighty God. Isaiah continues to say in verse 28: 'Have you not known? Have you not heard? The Lord is the everlasting God, the creator of the ends of the earth. He does not faint or grow weary.' He is the source and originator of power. He is the resource and the generator of all power. Isaiah continues in verses 29–31: 'He gives power to the faint, and to him who has no might he increases strength. Even youths shall faint and be weary, and young men shall fall exhausted; but they who wait for the Lord shall renew their strength.'

Our Lord Jesus, coming back from the grave with the keys of death and hell, saying 'All power is given to me in heaven and earth' (Matthew 28:18). And in Luke 10:19: 'Behold I give you power to tread on serpents and scorpions, and over all the power of the enemy.' He continues in Acts 1:8: 'But you shall receive power when the Holy Spirit has come upon you; and you shall be my witnesses . . . '

We shall be fruit producers, we shall do exploits by the power and the strength and enablement of this mighty being we call God. Matthew adds 'nothing shall be impossible unto you'. The Acts record continues:

When the day of Pentecost was fully come, they were all together in one place. And suddenly a sound came from heaven like the rush of a mighty wind, and it filled all the house where they were sitting. And there appeared to them tongues as of fire, distributed and resting on each one of them. And they were all filled with the Holy Spirit.

Rhinard Bunkie points out that each one had his own baptism, and each one had his own endowment of power. It was as though each one was given his own power station, they now had the potential, under God, to do the work of Christ, and greater works because Christ said 'Go unto the Father'.

Here we see no limitations or boundaries to the potential of the believer now filled with the Holy Spirit.

Thus, Peter, in Acts 3, when challenged about the lame man now healed, says 'Why look on us, the God of our Father hast glorified Jesus and through faith in His name, has made this man strong'. God made mankind in His own image and likeness and gave him dominion and authority so that he could be an extension of the abilities and the creative power of the Almighty God. He gave him the ability to succeed, to overcome and to be victorious, not to be a loser or defeated, and this power is available to His Church. In Colossians 3:10, we are told that we have put on the new man, which is being renewed in knowledge according to the original pattern of God, who created us. Ephesians 4:8 adds: 'When He ascended on high, He led captivity captive, and gave gifts unto men.'

Jesus' life and ministry was the biggest success story, both collectively and individually. The Church, then, is the workplace of God. The Church, then, is the workplace of the Holy Spirit. The Church coming together in one place is the body of Christ meeting to continue under the directorship of its head, Jesus Christ, who continues to dictate the works and the activities.

The Acts of the Apostles is the sample, it's the model, it's the type of Church which Christ wants to carry through its activities, and as you know, the Acts of the Apostles is one of only two books in the Bible that does not have an ending. It is the book of continuation. As long as Jesus Christ has a Church on earth, as long as there is one soul to be brought in, He will want the Church to continue the work discussed in Acts 1:1: 'Jesus began both to do and teach.'

The Holy Spirit is helping us to be moulded into the model that Christ wants us to be. He is interceding for us in our prayers and in our groaning that cannot be uttered. He is renewing and He is improving us everyday. In 2 Corinthians 3:18 the Bible says: 'And we all, with unveiled face, beholding the glory of the Lord, are being changed into his likeness from one degree of glory to another.' We have the potential therefore to succeed both as a Church and as individuals. Let me ask you 'how do you see your Church in five years' time?' Are you satisfied with the growth rate or with developments? Are you satisfied with the quality of worship? Are you satisfied with the expansion and the extensions in the Church? If you are not, then I have good news for you, you are in good company. Jesus Christ is pouring out His Spirit upon His Church in an unprecedented manner in fulfilment of the prophecies of scripture. Our co-operation with God does not mean having to nurse a Church of ten, fifteen or twenty members. If we would open our minds to do some big thinking, some big planning, some big praying and have big expectations, God will honour His word and we will see His glory. We now have the potential to achieve and to succeed, to bless and to be a blessing, to prosper and to see our children prosper, to become employers instead of employees, to become masters instead of servants, to prosper and be in good health, even as our souls prosper, and to walk in safety and in security. Deuteronomy 28:10 adds: 'The people of the earth shall see the difference that the blessings and the anointing of God makes upon our life.'

It is also true that many of us from our cultural background, from our circumstantial background, have learned to think small. To plan small, to expect small things, to be satisfied with the mediocre, to be satisfied with less than the best. The scriptures today are calling us to the place of co-operation and partnership with God, for the Bible says 'we are workers, we are partners together with God. We are God's business, we are God's husbandry, we are God's workmanship, and we are God's finished product.' This God wants to show Himself strong. How does He show Himself strong? He shows Himself strong through Jesus Christ, through His Church and through individuals like you and I. Arise and possess our possessions. We are God's finished product. When the tradesman has finished the furniture, he would select the best piece and put it on show so that people who pass and see would know the quality and the ability of his work by that finished product. That is what God seeks to do with us. To select those of us that will exercise faith, those of us that will show obedience, those of us who will discipline our minds, our hearts, our bodies and our thinking, to co-operate with Him so that He may shine through us. We are His workmanship, we are His finished product that we may show forth who He really is. We should be able to say 'if you want to know what God is like, look at Jesus. If you want to know what Jesus is like, look at the Church. If you want to know what the Church should be like, look at us.'

In the secular world, mankind co-operates with God's laws and does exploits. Man makes a jet to fly faster than the speed of sound. He makes an aeroplane to carry more than a thousand passengers; he has walked on the moon; he has landed probes on Mars; he has made breakthroughs in medicine, in education, in industries, all fulfilling the prophetic word of God in Daniel 12.

The Church must rise up to its full potential and fulfil the prophecies of Joel 2. Many of us have given up hope, but I have news for you today, we are the sons of God, we are the children of the most High.

LIVING OUT OF VISION

Philip Mohabir

Philip was born in Guyana and at the age of 15 became the only Christian in his Hindu village. After eight years in England as a missionary in the 1950s and 1960s, he returned to his homeland and for nineteen years pioneered evangelism and church planting throughout Guyana and the Caribbean, establishing over 100 churches. Since moving to the UK in 1983, he has been committed to building bridges between black and white Christians. He is the founder and president of the African and Caribbean Evangelical Alliance and a vice president of the Evangelical Alliance. He oversees the International Christian Leadership Connections (ICLC) Network and leads the UK-based Connections ministry. His book *Building Bridges* (Hodder & Stoughton, 1988) and the video *Philip Mohabir — Fisher of Men* (CV6 Television, 1992) tell his story. His mandate — 'Take the gospel of Christ to the different people'.

KEY SCRIPTURES: ACTS 26:12–20; 1:3;
PROVERBS 29:18; ISAIAH 6:1–8;
HEBREWS 11:7–16

Paul said: 'Consequently I was not *disobedient* to the heavenly *vision.*'

Solomon said: 'Where there is *no vision* the people perish . . .' Where there is no one to see, the people will be unrestrained. (Uncontrollable chaos, ungovernable, without boundaries, no recognized lines of distinction, each one left to make their own rules and do what seems right in his/her own eyes, inevitable self-destruction, PERISH.)

77

Whenever the Church loses its ability to see, it automatically loses its prophetic cutting edge. With no prophet to watch and warn, to discern and declare, to envision and encourage, the doors/gates of the city are left unguarded and unprotected. They are wide open for enemy infiltration and invasion. ENTER greyness, complacency, comfort, ease, compromise, and soft options, in other words lukewarmness. EXIT clarity, focus, and a sense of purpose and destiny. The bold spirit of the pioneer is imperceptibly reduced to the inertia of a settler. The willingness to take risks is unintentionally coerced into the paralysis of comfort zones. The excitement and joy derived from the certain knowledge that we are GOD'S COVENANT PEOPLE called and committed to build CHURCH according to the New Testament pattern, gives way to a sad, dull and heavy drudgery. When the heart of the Church is no longer captivated by passionate vision to be A RADICAL KINGDOM PEOPLE committed to a KINGDOM AGENDA, then it is inevitable that we will not, indeed we cannot, impact the world powerfully enough to make a difference.

Obedience to God-given vision ensures success, growth and victory but disobedience leads to defeat and disgrace. Saul plunged the whole nation of Israel into a period of darkness, frustration and defeat because he rejected prophetic instructions and directions. Israel's kings prospered whenever they submitted to the influence of the prophets (seers), but were led unwilling captives and slaves to live and work under the tyranny of a pagan society, and serve an alien king, when they resisted.

We cannot afford to ignore prophetic vision but rather ensure that our personal and corporate life complies with the expressed desires of God and that our agendas are in strict alignment with the declared KINGDOM PURPOSE for this generation. 'He who has ears to hear, let him/her hear what the Spirit is saying to the churches.' He/she who has eyes to see what God is revealing and doing, let him/her follow where the Spirit is leading. To discern divine direction is to determine our destiny. There is a desperate urgency for us to recapture a vision of (1) the Church, (2) the lost unreached and unevangelized millions, (3) the future, and (4) the Kingdom and the King.

Vision of Church

Jesus said 'I will build my church and the gates of hell shall not prevail against it' (Matthew 16:18). Jesus loves the Church, and died for her, He is the head of the Church, and provides all the Church needs to experience full salvation. He sanctifies her, preparing her for a great presentation coronation (Ephesians 5:23–27). The Church is important to Jesus and very crucial to His redemptive purpose for humankind. It holds a significant place in God's thinking. It is central to the fulfilment of Kingdom Purposes.

I believe in the Church. There is no substitute. God has no 'B' plan. The Church is the God-appointed AGENCY to fulfil His Kingdom agenda for planet earth, to manifest his wisdom, power and glory to powers and principalities in heavenly places. The Church is GOD'S AUTHENTIC ALTERNATIVE for a spiritually and morally exhausted bankrupt world (Ephesians 3:10). The MISSION of the Church is to reflect/mirror the Father-heart of God for a sad, broken and bleeding world. We are salt, light and city set on a hill (Matthew 5:13–14).

If the Church will realize its full potential to reach the nations of the world with the gospel of the kingdom, to challenge sin and evil within and without, to bring healing to the nations and to impact our world sufficiently to change the destiny of future generations, then we need to rediscover true APOSTOLIC ANOINTING in terms of its life, character, practices and mission. It is high time for us to cut through the jungle of religious unreality: theological rhetoric and traditional paraphernalia, in order to re-establish in our experience true SPIRITUALITY and actual spiritual AUTHORITY.

Oh that we will stop playing Church and in earnest be Church as the Father designed it. The one element absolutely essential to ensure effective apostolic life, function, community and ministry is the release of the complementary combination of *apostolic authority and prophetic vision.*

What is CHURCH?

> The chosen and anointed messianic community totally submitted to the lordship of Christ, sent out on an ambassadorial mission to proclaim Christ as crucified, risen, glorified and coming King, as good news to every people group regardless of geography, ethnicity, culture or language.

As the man said:

Vision without action = visionary
Action without vision = activist drudgery
Vision with action = missionary.

Vision just for the sake of it is a very unfruitful exercise. Vision, which does not motivate and stimulate you into action, is words without works, talk without action, ideas without initiative and dreams without fulfilment. Jude calls it clouds without water. No substance . . . a waste of time. Action without vision is a legalistic obedience, faithful though it may be, driven by a sense of duty or wanting to prove worthy of approval, or even fear of failing God. Our vision should be a response of love to Him who first loved us.

Observe the following scriptures: Acts 9:1–9; 26:12–20.

1. True vision is born out of a genuine personal encounter with the risen Christ.
2. True vision will impact your life sufficiently to rearrange your priorities and alter the course of events forever. You will never be the same again.
3. True vision is the risen Lord imparting and implanting His heart and spirit into your heart and spirit.
4. True vision is not humanly conceived or perceived. It is not the process of intellectual discourse or debate.
5. It is the ability to discern the mind of God and to experience the heart of God.

6. True vision originates in heaven, not earthly but heavenly, an 'out of this world experience' (2 Corinthians 12:1–5).
7. True vision is directly related to Kingdom concerns (Acts 1:3).
8. True vision is directly linked to faith and obedience.

Noah built the Ark because he had a revelation of things not yet seen. Abraham stepped out into the unknown in obedience to the call of God because he caught a glimpse of the eternal city not made with hands. Sarah received ability to conceive and bear a son far beyond her natural capabilities. Isaiah saw the Lord resplendent in all His glory and his entire life and his ministry was completely transformed. Abraham's faith extended far beyond death because his heart burnt with a vision of the unknown.

True vision is not:

1. The dreams, hopes or the aspirations of a godly person. Whatever their virtue, unless they are rooted in the purposes of God, they can become daydreams (unreal). They often prove to be a distraction, unproductive, energy-sapping exercise void of any Holy Spirit content. End results — forever chasing the rainbow.
2. The ambitions of the child of God, however sanctified and well-meaning.
3. The conclusions reached after going through the process of discussion and debate.
4. The carefully drawn-out recommendations made after psychoanalysis of the social, economical, moral and stress factors of the individual, church or house group.
5. The occasional prophecy, word of knowledge or revelation, necessarily, especially if they bear no relation to where the body as a whole is going. (Outside body context.)
6. The carefully devised plans and programmes after due consideration is given to the problems, cost, availability of manpower and appropriate resources.
7. The agenda based on noble ideas or sound management principles.

8. The seeking after the flavour of the month, newest fad, revelation or experience.

Good and legitimate as these things are, however full of spiritual value and virtue, and one must not deny their validity to the Christian life and work, they do not constitute vision from God that fills the heart with a consuming passion to spend and be spent for Kingdom concerns, to pursue radical holiness with a vengeance and to fully fill our APOSTOLIC mandate. We need to rise from our present level of sub-normal Christianity and allow the resurrected Christ and Holy Spirit to elevate us to throne level, where the triumphant Christ is seated far above all powers and principalities.

Can you not hear the call from the throne? Who will be cleansed? Who will be touched with fresh fire from the throne altar? Who will go to the nations? (Isaiah 6:1–8). Come up higher!

Quality of the vision we need

The vision we need:

1. Is the kind which comes by being alone with the Lord in intimate communion, lingering in His holy presence, offering the sacrifice of praise in the deep inner sanctuary where the Shekinah glory fills the temple, there to enjoy waves of refreshing divine energy and to behold His exquisite beauty filled with ecstasy, to be lifted and transported as it were on the wings of the Spirit, far away and above the ugly stressfulness of daily humdrum and hassle, into the awesomeness of His world.
2. Is when the Lord draws back the curtain of time and allows us to peep into the invisible and eternal realities of the heavenly.
3. Is when the God of our Lord Jesus Christ, the Father of Glory, opens the eyes of our heart and enlightens our

understanding: to fully grasp the *hope* to which we are called in Christ; that we, His covenant blood-bought precious people, are His glorious riches and inheritance (Ephesians 1:16; 2:6); to reveal the surpassing greatness of His resurrection power invested in us; to comprehend that we are *destined to throne position* in Christ to reign.

4. Is laying open our hearts so that he can share the deep concerns and burdens that are on His heart, to permit Him to impart into our spirits His purposes.

5. Is when the Spirit of the Lord takes us beyond the finite limitedness and fragility of our own humanity and enable us to discern the differences between divine/human, eternal/temporal, endures/fades, incorruptible/corruptible, immortal/mortal, strong/weak, rich/poor, good/evil, of God/of the devil.

6. Is when the Holy Spirit gives us prophetic insight into situations closed to human discovery, reveals the deep secrets of the human heart, exposes sin and evil hidden in the deep recesses of darkness.

7. Is when the Holy Spirit catapults us into the future to show things that will come to pass. He gives insight and foresight, thus equipping us with the facts so that on the one hand we can encourage, comfort and warn the people, and on the other hand enabling us to retain and maintain focus and right perspective.

8. Is when the Holy Spirit helps to understand what our true potential and possibilities are in Christ, and stimulates our faith to tackle the impossible and reach for the powers of the age to come (Hebrews 6:5).

9. Is when the Lord delivers us from our own sense of importance and egocentricity, releases us from the smallness of our own concerns, helps us realize that the world does not revolve around us and our gifts, abilities and ministries.

10. Is when the Lord liberates us from the trivia and pettiness of our own frame of reference and brings us into the larger more important place of the redemptive purposes of God for lost humanity.

When our hearts are captivated with a vision of this nature like Abraham, Daniel, Moses, David, Paul, Stephen, Peter, Sadhu Sundar Singh, Watchman Nee, Bhengu, Hudson Taylor, C. T. Studd and other unsung heroes of our faith, our lives will be transformed forever, our vistas will be lifted, our horizons expanded, our daring stirred up to attempt the impossible to conquer new worlds, and to do exploits far beyond our capabilities and resources.

Advantageous benefits

There are distinct advantages to any individual believer or church community who has a clearly defined mission statement. Everyone needs a definite understanding of God's DESIGN, PURPOSE and WILL. 'For the Kingdom of God to come His will must be done.' For His will to be done we must know it, believe it and do it. We must order our lives to live in total submission to His authority and surrender our highest ambition to be governed by the word of God and the Spirit of God irrespective of the cost or consequences. If it is true that without vision we perish then it must follow that with vision we prosper. Here are some benefits to the Christian as I see it.

1. *Motivation*: Vision motivates. Once we see the God of glory, and once the heart is captivated by a vision of the general assembly of saints and the Church of the first born enrolled in heaven, and we realize that we have come to Mount Zion, and the Judge of all, and to the spirits of just men made perfect, and to Jesus, the mediator of the new covenant, and to the sprinkled blood, which speaks better things than that of Abel (Hebrews 1:10; 12:22–24), we cannot turn back, doubt, waver or tremble on the brink. Like Abraham we will believe in spite of all the odds stacked up against us. We will await His good pleasure in spite of contradicting circumstances. Long after the evening sun has disappeared beyond the distant horizon, when all hope is gone and the impossible looms larger than ever, we will still

dare to trust. We will not give way to fear and doubt, and if need be we die still trusting, because we know that what we have seen is real. It is not a fake, He in whom we believe is not a disappointment. It is real, not an empty dream. Motivated by a vision of our eternal prospect, we cannot adopt a *laissez-faire* attitude waiting for things to happen, but make things happen.

2. *Stimulation*: Vision stimulates our faith. It builds our confidence to trust God implicitly because it does not rest on the good ideas, persuasive words and philosophies of men, but is rooted in the wisdom and the power of God (1 Corinthians 2:4–5). Our security is firmly anchored in God's love and His plans for our welfare, not for our calamity but to give future and hope (Jeremiah 29:11).

3. *Encouragement*: Vision encourages the faint, discouraged, disillusioned, wounded, weary, tired and burnt-out pilgrim. We have this treasure in earthen vessels, and as such we suffer distresses, dishonour, lack of appreciation, sorrow and pain (2 Corinthians 4:7–10; 6:1–10). We are all vulnerable. No one has yet been promoted to the status of superwoman/man. Whatever our rank, we all need to be commended and affirmed. Yet in spite of the fragility of our human nature we are assured that we will not be crushed, destroyed or forsaken. We will not despair because we know who we are and what we have in Christ. We know that the Father is committed to His will and word. 'God is not a man that He should lie or repent, has He not said and will He not do it? Or has He not spoken and will he not make it good?' (Numbers 23:19). God does not play games with us. Where He guides He provides. He stands by what He commands. What He reveals He also fulfils. God is committed to the heavenly blueprint. He does not repent of His plans and purposes. He gives us the strength to go on when our own strength is gone. 'Faithful is He who calls you and He also will bring it to pass' (1 Thessalonians 5:24).

4. *Direction:* Vision helps us to keep on course, keeps our focus fixed on the important and avoids us concentrating on the urgent, prevents majoring on the minors and inspires us to spend our energies on the essentials instead of the non-essentials. If we see clearly the ultimate, where we should go, if our hearts are set to follow the Lamb wherever He leads, and if we are determined to accomplish His declared mandate, then the enemy will not be able to easily divert or distract us from God's chosen path for our lives. In the event that we stray, a vision of the ultimate goal will enable us to re-adjust and re-align. The heart, which burns with vision of God's blueprint, will always pay close attention to the details of design and hold as paramount the instructions given. We will want above all else to please our Lord by building to His pattern. Like Moses and Noah, to finish all the work 'just as the Lord commanded' (Exodus 40).

VISION WILL KEEP US ON TRACK and act as a plumbline by which we can then measure our progress and evaluate the quality of our work. Let us never forget the wise words of Paul: 'Let each man/woman be careful how he/she builds; each man's/woman's work will become evident; for the day will show it, because it is to be revealed with fire; and the fire itself will test the quality of each man's/woman's work' (1 Corinthians 3:10, 13).

Essential vision

Let us take heart: the Holy Spirit will work in us and through us to do all that is required of us. He is given to be our Paraclete to enlighten, equip, enable and empower us to be the faithful stewards and able servants of the new covenant. The Church is the appointed instrument in the hand of God to stem the rising tide of evil, to bring light into the sur-rounding darkness and pull down the strongholds of Satan in our midst. To effectively do so we need to:

1. *Have a fresh vision of God.* My God is only as great and wonderful as my perception of Him. We desperately need to

lift the limitations we place on God. He is far bigger than our creativity or imagination. We need to have a fresh appreciation of our heavenly Father. The Santa Claus subjective image of God is not enough. To sustain daring and dynamic faith, to maintain the excitement in our spirit or to feed the unquenchable fires of love and undying devotion, or to keep the springs of irresistible joy ever flowing, we need to see that God is far higher than the subjectivity of our own meagre experiences or needs. We need to balance the subjective with an objective view of the ALMIGHTY. Like Isaiah, we need to see Him sitting on His Throne, lofty and exalted, to appreciate His transcendence, far removed from the things of time and space, far above the wretchedness and ugliness of this present evil age, untouched, unspoilt beauty and purity. God who is Sovereign and sufficient, a God who is not intimidated, threatened or taken by surprise by sin, Satan, circumstances or change. We need to have a fresh vision and appreciation of the true God.

Transcendent	yet	Immanent;
Incomprehensible	yet	Comprehensible;
Awesome Holiness	yet	Amazing Grace and Abundant Mercy;
Great Love	yet	Great Compassion;
God of Infinity	yet	God of the Incarnation;

Full of splendour, glory, honour, might, majesty, power, riches, dominion and praises forever and ever.

Oh how we need to enlarge our vision of the everlasting Almighty, Father of glory, Father of the Lord Jesus Christ, my Father, your Father.

2. *A fresh vision of ourselves*: a fresh vision of who we are and what we have in Christ. Too often we live below and beneath our calling. We need to take our place in the Kingdom as His heirs and joint-heirs. To be secured in our identity in Christ. To enjoy our riches and blessings in Christ in heavenly places and not remain in our poverty-syndrome. He has placed at our disposal the unlimited riches, power and

authority of the throne. We need to re-assert our rightful authority given to us by the risen Lord. We are called to be partners with Christ to change the world, build the Church, and extend the Kingdom by making disciples of all nations. We are destined to lead the way by being God's demonstration models, setting the trends, to be the head and not the tail. We are the salt of the earth, the light of the world, Jesus said (Matthew 5:13 and 14). Paul said we are given the ministry of reconciliation (2 Corinthians 5:19). We need a fresh realization of the rich deposit and the gospel of glory God has entrusted us. For this the world awaits. Rise to the challenge of the hour and take your place.

3. *A fresh vision of God's design for Church.* The Lord has not delegated the building of His Church to human wisdom and ingenuity. He does not borrow from any social, political or cultural systems and structures. His design is unique and original. He purposed in Himself after His own counsel and good pleasure of His will (Ephesians 1:9–14). Jesus said 'I will build my church'. Its composition, purpose, government, mission, structures, ministries come from the depths of His own eternal being. Nothing is left to the imagination. Each detail is carefully, meticulously stamped with the nature of the divine.

Church was never meant to be institutional in character but always to be relational. Never a high-powered organization but an organism. A dynamic community of believers. Individuals who are born again finding their right place as set by the Lord within the corporate whole. We need to return in experience and practice to the BODY CONCEPT OF THE CHURCH. There is great need to rediscover and restore the missing ingredients to church life and practice. Such indispensable and irreplaceable elements are RELATIONSHIP based on mutual acceptance of each other; covenant commitment; common care; loyalty and trust, and more than words and experiments.

DIVERSITY in UNITY cannot remain a pipe dream, but must be more than something to endure until it is no longer convenient. We must be willing to put things right with each other, forgive, confess, and pray for one another. The dividing walls of gender, race, culture, prejudices must be pulled down. *No room* for the 'better than you', 'holier than you' spirit.

SUBMISSION to spiritual authority that is biblical, radical and based on proper practice, without abuse, must not only be endlessly debated but demonstrated in real-life situations.

SOLIDARITY . . . the idea of the many being one. One for the many and the many for the one must be worked out in reality and without partiality. Our sense of belonging and a common identity must now go beyond religious jargon and be demonstrated in real-life situations.

ASCENSION MINISTRY GIFTS need more than ever to function in the context of TEAM to complement one another, so that their combined ministry and accumulated anointing lift the Church to a higher level of maturity, and usher in a new apostolic era.

GIFTS OF THE SPIRIT . . . these power tools given to equip the saints to do greater works and demonstrate the power of God to a sceptical unbelieving world that the gospel of the Kingdom is not a words-only message. Miracles, signs and wonders are still relevant. Isn't it time we take the exercise of these powerful gifts outside of our comfort zones, of cosy, safe charismatic circles, to the streets, to the non-Christian world? Incidentally, can you explain why the same few people always function in the same three or four gifts in every meeting?

NEW TESTAMENT CHURCH GOVERNMENT . . . we need to have a new look at leadership issues in our churches. Some leaders have not grown with their congregation. Others are burnt-out and need a refreshing, reappraisal and, who knows, a change of function. Yet again we may have faithful women and men functioning outside the measure of their calling and gifting. We may need to do some serious sorting out, re-ordering priorities, resetting agendas. However painful it may be, let us bear the pain and pay the price that every pruning session demands, so that in the long run we may be more productive. The alternative does not warrant consideration. We may wake up to discover that we have built contrary to God's design. A radical Church is only as radical as its leaders. Let us be radical enough to set things in order as Paul instructed Titus. Appoint only such people who will allow Jesus to remain Head of his Church. Let us ask some questions. What kind of leadership structure do you have in your church? Is it biblical or is it inherited from some pagan religious mixture system of the past? By what criteria do you judge their suitability? Do they fulfil the conditions for spiritual leadership as set out in the scriptures?

4. *A fresh mission vision*: the primary task of the Church is to communicate the gospel of the Kingdom to every creature. There is still an unfinished task. In the present move of the Spirit new hope for revival has been born in the hearts of many of us. Whilst we are experiencing and enjoying the phenomena, let us not allow ourselves to be lulled into a false sense of security, worse yet, to become so self-indulgent that we forget the two-thirds of the world's population which is still unevangelized; and the 11,000 unreached people groups; the 10/40 window; inner-city desolation, the disadvantaged, broken millions; 90-plus per cent of the UK, non-church people. It will require the involvement of the whole Church to take the whole gospel to the whole world (Billy Graham). We need to catch a vision of the multitudes that are distressed, downcast, sheep without a shepherd, poor, captives, blind and lost. When Jesus saw them He was moved with compassion. Can we not cultivate a new culture of faith and expectation to a nation-wide revival that will sweep the masses into the kingdom? God is not finished yet. Let us rise to answer the Lord, 'here am I Lord; send me'.

5. *A fresh vision of the Eternal City*: John saw the Eternal City coming down from God out of heaven; it shone with the glory of God, like a jasper clear and transparent; it had a great wall. Its origin and nature is God. This city is the greatest and most influential in the whole universe; kings of the earth bring their splendour into it. Its citizens live in the unending day of God's glory and the light that streams from

the Lamb. If we are gripped by the vision of this city we can never settle for anything less. It will affect how we worship, labour, how we build, how we pray, how we relate with those who share the vision and those who don't.

6. *A fresh vision of the Cross*: the Cross should always remain central. Our vision of the Cross should never be clouded by circumstances, cares, compromise, sin, grief, disappointments, bereavement, illness, personal loss of status or shame, for in the Cross lies our hope and salvation. The vision of it should never grow dim. Its true meaning and significance to the Christian gospel can never be exaggerated. As such therefore we cannot afford to dilute its contents, diminish its value or compromise its message. No Cross no healing, no forgiveness, no freedom from guilt and condemnation, no cleansing, no justice, and no liberty for the captives, no reconciliation, no redemption . . . no message of hope.

To fully appreciate the love and grace of God, the utter wretchedness of sin, the magnanimity and intensity of Jesus' sacrifice, the extent of God's judgement poured against sin, and our own absolute helplessness, we need to remember the Lamb without spot, crucified, hanging there as our substitute. How could He love us so? Paul said 'By the preaching of the cross is the wisdom and power of God, we preach CHRIST and him crucified. I am determined to know nothing among you except CHRIST AND HIM CRUCIFIED.' May we never surrender to the temptation to sideline the Cross but let us return to boldly preach it and restore its centrality in our worship, prayers, teaching, programme agendas. I know most of us have paid the price to be radical pioneers. We have dreamt that things would have progressed further. Maybe you have been disappointed, hurt, disillusioned, find it hard to continue, a wounded brother/sister. Remember the race is not over, remember it takes time to reach the ultimate from the immediate. God has an ultimate for His Church . . . It is a glorious, triumphant CHURCH.

It is time we really start believing what we say we believe. Do we believe in unity, relationship, solidarity, harmony, spiritual authority? Then how is there so much division, strife, insecurity, disharmony, walking away from each other and rebellion? Are we serious, or sick, or something? Do you think we need to do some repenting and putting things right with each other?

DOUBLE FOR ALL YOUR SINS

Reverend Donald W. McFarlane

Reverend Donald McFarlane was born on 28 July 1951, in Portland, Jamaica. He attended Titchfield High and Portland High Secondary School. He later received a Bachelor of Arts degree in Theology and a Master's in Religious Studies.

Donald has served in several capacities since 1973 to the present time. From 1973 to 1978 he served as pastor/evangelist in Kingston, Jamaica. In 1978 he was invited to serve as pastor/evangelist for the Seventh-day Adventist Church in Britain. From 1978 to 1981 he served as the minister of Handsworth Seventh-day Adventist Church, Birmingham. Donald was also the minister of Camp Hill Seventh-day Adventist Church, Birmingham from 1981 to 1984. He was Secretary of the North British Conference of the Seventh-day Adventist Church in 1984, and Secretary of the British Union Conference in 1985. He served as British Union Secretary from 1985 to 1991. He was elected President of the South England Conference of the Seventh-day Adventist Church in 1991.

Donald is currently the South England Conference President and has administrative and pastoral responsibilities for 122 congregations within the Seventh-day Adventist Church.

KEY SCRIPTURE: ISAIAH 40:1, 2 AV

Comfort ye, comfort ye my people, saith your God. Speak ye comfortably to Jerusalem, and cry unto her, that her warfare is accomplished, that her iniquity is pardoned; for she hath received of the Lord's hand double for all her sins.

The prophet Isaiah lived in a troubled world. It was a time of peril and crisis for Israel, for God's people. It was a time of material prosperity but also a time of spiritual decline. Justice was in short supply as magistrates judged for rewards, and rulers were more interested in personal gain than the welfare of the people. The rich became richer and the poor poorer. Many sank into the depths of poverty and were reduced to the status of slaves. In general, the people clung to the outward forms of religion but knew nothing of its meaning and power.

Isaiah warned Israel that such conditions could not long endure. God would put an end to the unacceptable conditions by severely punishing them. At the same time, Isaiah outlined God's love for His erring people in words of deep tenderness.

The book of Isaiah can be divided into three distinct sections:

Section 1: chapters 1–35. Here we have a series of denunciations against transgressions and pronouncements of judgement, which would be poured out upon Israel because of her rebelliousness.

Section 2: chapters 36–39. These chapters foretell the invasion of Israel by the Babylonians, as well as the illness and recovery of King Hezekiah.

Section 3: chapters 40–66. Here we see God's outpouring of grace upon repentant Israel. These chapters are full of God's promises of forgiveness, predictions of the coming of the Messiah, and what He would do at His coming. And thus we have passages such as Isaiah 53, which portrays the Messiah as the sin-bearer: 'He was wounded for our transgressions; He was bruised for our iniquities. The chastisement of our peace was upon Him and with His stripes we are healed' (Isaiah 53:3). And then there is Isaiah 55:1, 'Ho, everyone that thirsteth, come ye to the water, and he that hath no money, come ye buy and eat; yea, come, buy wine and milk without money and without price'. Isaiah 40 – 66 has earned for the prophet Isaiah the name 'the Gospel Prophet' or the Good News prophet. The eloquence of these passages demonstrates with irrefutable evidence that they had their source in the mind of the divine.

Now let's look again at our text, Isaiah 40:1 and 2: 'Comfort ye, comfort ye my people, saith your God. Speak ye comfortably to Jerusalem, and cry unto her, that her warfare is accomplished, that her iniquity is pardoned: for she hath received of the Lord's hand double for all her sins.' These are tender words, kind words, words of a loving Father. Of particular importance is the expression in verse 2 'For she hath received of the Lord's hand *double for all her sins*'. This is a statement the context of which suggests that it is loaded with weighty significance for God's people, but its meaning is not readily apparent. It is nevertheless a term with which the prophets and their hearers were familiar, in that it is mentioned in other places in scripture. For example Isaiah 61:7 says: 'For your shame ye shall have double; and for confusion they shall rejoice in their portion: therefore in their land they shall possess the double: everlasting joy shall be unto them.' And Zechariah 9:12 says: 'Turn ye to the strong hold, ye prisoners of hope: even today do I declare that I will render double unto thee.' In both Isaiah 61:7 and Zechariah 9:12, the giving of double is stated as something positive. Whatever it was, it was designated to bring joy to a people who previously had experienced God's wrath against sin.

Some have understood 'double' to mean double punishment for sin, but that is unlikely. If Zechariah 9:12 means 'I will render double punishment unto thee', that would not be a reason for joy and hope but for gloom and depression. Others say that 'double' could mean double forgiveness, an expression of how thoroughly God has forgiven His people. This seems closer to the point.

But there is a third option, and it seems to express most eloquently the prophet's account of God's forgiveness. In the days of Isaiah, if one owed a large debt which he was unable to pay, more likely than not he would be required to turn his home and property over to his creditor. It was an extremely embarrassing situation. The debtor had to leave his home with his wife and children. The creditor would place a notice on the main door of the house listing the man's debts. Anyone was free to go up to the door to read the notice. A loss of dignity, a loss of status, a loss of face.

There were two ways for the debtor to have his house returned to him:

1. The property would be returned in the year of Jubilee.

And ye shall hallow the fiftieth year, and proclaim liberty throughout all the land unto all the inhabitants thereof; it shall be a jubilee unto you and ye shall return every man unto his possession, and ye shall return every man unto his family. A jubilee shall that fiftieth year be unto you; ye shall not sow, neither reap that which groweth of itself in it, nor gather the grapes in it of thy vine undressed. For it is the jubilee; it shall be holy unto you: ye shall eat the increase thereof out of the field. In the year of this jubilee ye shall return every man unto his possession. (Leviticus 25:10–13)

2. The second way in which the man and his family could have his house returned to them was to have someone pay the debt — a relative, a friend or just a kind person. When the debt was settled by a third party, that person would then go up to the door and fold the offending document in two, 'doubling it', in order to hide the statement of debt. That act of doubling declared that the debt had been paid. The former debtor was free to return home. This was a source of great joy for the debtor. *He had received double.* Freed from the shackles of the debt, he was back in a right relationship with his creditor.

The custom of doubling is practised today in certain Jewish communities.

It is a happy custom in some Jewish quarters of great cities for a wealthy Jew to seek out needy compatriots and try to help them. Up and down the streets of the ghetto he goes, scanning each door for a telltale white paper fluttering in the breeze. At last he sees one. It is a bill, which the tenant of the cottage cannot pay. Going softly to the door the would-be benefactor withdraws it, takes it to the creditor and pays the bill in full. Then folding the receipt bill in half (doubling), he again tiptoes to the door and pins it where he found it. With what happiness the poor bankrupt discovers the next morning that his debt is fully paid. (Ransome W. Cooper in A. Naismith, *1200 More Notes, Quotes and Anecdotes* (Pickering & Inglis, London, 1975), p. 59)

'You have received double for all your sins' was music to the ears of the children of Israel. God had forgiven them and covered up their sin. We too have received double for our sins. The penalty for our sins was not merely the loss of our homes but the eternal loss of our lives — so clearly stated by St Paul in Romans 6:23: 'For the wages of sin is death.'

The pages of history are littered with the heroic acts of men and women who gave their lives for others. Friends have given their lives for friends. Mothers for daughters, and fathers for sons. But there was no human being good enough to give his life to save us from the death caused by sin. All the oil in the Middle East could not pay for our sins. But God sent his Son Jesus into our world to become man, and as a man, sinless man, to pay the penalty for our sins by His death that we could be saved from eternal death. No wonder John 3:16 declares: 'For God so loved the world that he gave his only begotten son that whosoever believeth in him should not perish but have everlasting life.'

When Jesus died on the cross that fateful Friday afternoon, He died not for Himself or for any sin which He had committed. His death was the ultimate sacrifice given for each human being. Christ died to pay the penalty for our sin, that wherein we were under the sentence of death we may now have everlasting life.

Therefore as by the offence of one judgement came upon all men to condemnation; even so by the righteousness of one, the free gift came upon all men unto justification

97

of life. For as by one man's disobedience many were made sinners, so by the obedience of one shall many be made righteous. That as sin hath reigned unto death, even so might grace reign through righteousness unto eternal life by Jesus Christ our Lord. (Romans 5:18, 19, 21)

Jesus offers us double for our sins. Whatever the mistakes of the past, however much we have messed up our lives He offers to cover up our sins. By His death He has paid the penalty for our sins. This is a source of joy.

Not only was Christ's death on Calvary a payment for our sin, it was also a demonstration of the value which God places on each human being. He values us so highly that He was willing for His only son to die for us. On the cross we see God's tangible expression of love.

One may say 'If Jesus died that we might live, why are we still dying?' You see the death that Jesus died to save us from is not that which we see around us each day: death from old age, accidents, and sickness. Such death the Bible calls a sleep from which we will be wakened when Christ returns to earth. 'For the trumpet shall sound and the dead in Christ shall rise first' (1 Corinthians 15:52). The death from which He died to save us is eternal death, eternal destruction, the death described by John in Revelation 20:14, 15: 'And death and hell were cast into the lake of fire. This is the second death. And whosoever was not found written in the book of life was cast into the lake of fire.' God has made us for life — eternal life. He desires that we share eternity with Him. To do so each one of us needs to accept the 'double' (the payment for our sins) which Jesus offers us. That's all He asks. It is a simple act of faith, but without acceptance we cannot receive it.

Recently I read about an ingenious scheme devised by Lord Congleton to teach the tenants on his estate how by faith they could receive forgiveness of sin, but be shut out from God's Kingdom through unbelief. Nearly all of his tenants were behind in their payments. Some of them were so far behind that they feared being thrown out of their homes. Congleton, to the astonishment of his tenants, posted a notice all over the estate promising remission of rent to any tenant who would meet with him in his office between certain stated hours on a particular day. The tenants were suspicious of Lord Congleton and spent the intervening days trying to find out what trick he was up to. On the appointed day Lord Congleton sat in his office awaiting the tenants' response to his generous offer, but the tenants were still outside discussing the offer. The hours fixed were 10 to 12 in the morning. Close to 12 o'clock a man who was unavoidably delayed rushed into Lord Congleton's office to claim the promised remission.

'Do you really expect your debt to be forgiven?' asked Lord Congleton.

'Indeed I do.'

'And why do you?' asked Congleton.

'Because your Lordship has promised.'

'And do you believe the promise?'

'Of course I do, my Lord.'

'Why?'

'Because your Lordship would not deceive a poor man.'

'But you are a good man, aren't you, conscientious and hardworking' said Lord Congleton.

'My Lord, your notice said nothing about that.'

'And so believing the notice and finding no conditions attached you have come for your receipt.'

'Yes my Lord.'

Lord Congleton wrote the receipt, gave it to the man, who waved it above his head and shouted 'I knew you wouldn't deceive us. God bless your Worship.' He was making for the door to show it to the other tenants but Congleton asked him to remain inside until the hour of 12 o'clock struck, since the promise of remission was based on faith. At 12 o'clock he marched out and waved his receipt, 'I've got it, my debt is cancelled'. Other tenants rushed to the office but found the door shut. Unbelief had kept them from having cancellation of their debt.

How sad it would be if that was said of us in relation to

Jesus' offer of 'double', his offer to cover up our sins and give us eternal life. 'I have heard thee in a time accepted, and in the day of salvation have I succoured thee. Behold, now is the accepted time; behold now is the day of salvation' (2 Corinthians 6:2).

I pray that you and I, like the wise tenant, will be able to shout 'I've got it; I've got it, my debt has been cancelled', not only when our Lord returns but here and now.

ENDINGS AND NEW BEGINNINGS

Reverend Delroy Hall

Reverend Delroy Hall was born on 12 July 1959. Delroy has one sister, Sandra. His mother, Dorothy, is 62 years old. Both his mother and sister have been committed Christians for a number of years. His father passed away nearly ten years ago. Together, his parents provided a stable home, a vibrant, effective Christian witness, and excellent role models for both Delroy and Sandra. By profession, Delroy is a counsellor. He began his training in psychotherapy in 1993.

Delroy accepted the Lord in February 1980, and became a member of the Church of God of Prophecy in Leicester on Sunday, 5 September 1982. He accepted the call into the ministry in 1994. He and his wife Paulette moved to Sheffield in August 1996 to pastor the Church of God of Prophecy at Duke Street, Sheffield. Prior to this assignment he was the pastor for the local Church of God of Prophecy in Leicester.

The background to this chapter is that it is the first sermon he preached a week after his installation as the new pastor of the Church of God of Prophecy, Duke Street, Sheffield. It was the first time many were to hear him share the word and he remembers commenting that it was too late to change their minds if they did not like his preaching.

KEY SCRIPTURE: MATTHEW 27:50–66

Jesus was crucified on the cross and in His final breath, He cried out and gave up the ghost. The subsequent events that took place were astonishing. The veil, the inner-dividing barrier of the Holy of Holies, was miraculously torn in two from top to bottom. The earth shook and the physical rocks broke in pieces. It is highly implausible that the earthquake coincided with the death of this special man. Other supernatural events took place. The graves opened and many that were dead came back to life. They wandered in the streets of Jerusalem and were seen by many inhabitants of the city.

The Roman military forces which were at the crucifixion of Jesus experienced these strange happenings. They were fearful and possibly considered that the man who they had just killed was the Son of God.

Women were in attendance at the death of Jesus, including Mary Magdalene, Mary the mother of James and John, and the mother of Zebedee's children. At night, a rich man by the name of Joseph came and asked if he could take the body of Jesus. Pilate consented. On receiving the body, Joseph wrapped it in a clean white cloth and laid it in a tomb. The entrance of the tomb was then sealed with a large boulder. After this, Joseph left the tomb, but very shortly afterwards the Bible informs us that the two Marys and the other Mary came nearby to the sepulchre where the body of Jesus was laid.

I am taken aback by the events which took place prior to the crucifixion, and also what happened the moment Jesus died. Questions arise in my thoughts. For example, what does it mean to give up the ghost?

Jesus' death brought a direct impact with the veil of the temple being torn. What did this represent? I believe that at His death, the barrier which prevented individuals, Jews and Gentiles, was no longer present, and humanity had access to God. No longer did man have to go via a high priest for his sins to be forgiven.

The ending of Jesus' earthly life brought about spiritual, physical and natural occurrences. There was the physical death of Jesus and the two other thieves who were crucified with Him. The spiritual implication was that the temple was affected.

The natural phenomena were that the earth shook and rocks broke, the sun and sky darkened, and many that had died gained life and walked the streets of the holy city,

Jerusalem. The death not only affected the before-mentioned but it also affected all mankind: 'truly this was the Son of God', said the Roman centurion.

The death of Jesus shook the earth, but one thing which is so tragic over this fact of history, is that the very people that He had ministered to for three years were nowhere to be found. Just imagine for a moment: He had eaten with them, saved them from difficult situations, taught them in such a way that their lives would never be the same again — and in his moment of need nobody was around to help Him.

Jesus' death was not a waste, and it was no ordinary death. He died according to the scriptures (Luke 24:44–47). His ending brought about the cessation of the old order, and ushered in a new beginning for humanity. It can be said that not all endings are good and not all beginnings are good either, but this was different. This ending, despite being gruesome, was good, but the beginning was even better.

Jesus was ministered to by the females; his funeral and burial arrangements were made by a stranger, but still no disciples . . .

It may be of interest just to be aware of the events which occurred on the morning of the crucifixion. The religious people were conspiring to get rid of Jesus. Eventually the Roman governor asked the people what was their pleasure. They demanded an exchange. The crowd shouted that they wanted Barabbas, who was a robber and a dishonest man. Pilate could not understand the logic of the people and washed his hands in the presence of the crowd to let them know that he was not going to take part in the execution of Jesus. After all, He had not done anything wrong.

The political, military and religious people publicly humiliated Jesus. His humiliation took the form of violence and public stripping. In His hour of torment, He was all on His own, possibly feeling left and isolated. In His pain and discomfort He had no companion. The man who was moved with compassion and mercy is left to suffer at the hands of His own people who showed none of the virtues which He displayed.

Imagine for a moment that someone whom you have spent some time with is tragically killed. How might you feel?

Jesus, their faithful leader, was now dead. There had been discussions previously as to who would take over the leadership, but no one was to take Jesus' place. There was a gap. In some organizations when a pastor leaves, a temporary pastor is installed, sometimes for up to two years until a permanent replacement is found. Unfortunately, at present our Church does not operate such a system but in the future it may. Today, the resident pastor has been taken on board.

The impact of Jesus' death was experienced differently by differing sets of people. The first group was the disciples. They had been with Jesus for three years. They had seen Him perform miracles, heal people, cleverly dispute with those who wanted to catch Him out. They had seen Him walk on water, calm the rough seas and miraculously feed five thousand people. He cared for them, loved them, and now He was nailed to a merciless cross, about to die. I am not sure how they may have felt, but I guess they may have felt angry, sad, scared and alone. Possibly, all types of thoughts would be spinning around in their heads. What would the future hold for them without Jesus? They possibly even felt deserted by Jesus.

The other group affected was the Marys. They followed Jesus at a distance but no doubt feeling sad that the one they had loved and cared for was now at the point of death.

The chief priests and the Pharisees were a group of people who no doubt would be glad to see the back of this subversive character. They were possibly feeling glad and anxious. 'At last we have got rid of Him. He has caused us too much trouble.'

Pilate, the governor, publicly washed his hands of the whole event. It has been debated that Pilate could have protested more vehemently, but he took the easiest option, that was to absolve himself 'of the blood of this innocent man' (Matthew 27:24b).

The next person influenced by this death was the Roman centurion: the sudden realization was that He (Jesus) was the

Son of God. My thinking is that at that moment God must have given the centurion some sort of understanding about this man who was hanging on this barbaric cross.

Finally, the absence of friends, the crisis of Christ, provided a means of opportunity for Joseph. He was wealthy and asked Pilate if he could take the body, and secondly, he was able to provide a tomb for Jesus. I am led to believe that the way the Chinese write 'crisis' means two things. The first aspect is 'danger' and the other side is 'opportunity'. For Joseph, this meant an opportunity to give service to God. Had the disciples been around, it is highly likely that he would not have played such an important role in this scene.

Maybe, there are some of you here today who fit into one of these categories. There may be other endings you are experiencing. Ending of jobs, ending of good health, ending of youth, ending of special relationships, maybe you have lost a loved one. The endings you experience will cause you to view life differently.

Many of you have grown attached to my predecessor over the years and you feel sad that he is going. That is okay, it is normal and perfectly natural. It is even okay if you call me by his name. I don't expect to suddenly arrive and for people to switch off just like that. Don't worry, I will not be offended.

The death of Jesus was not the end, because it brought in a new order for humanity. You and I now have direct access to the Father through Jesus. We no longer have to sacrifice numerous animals to be acceptable to God. He accepts us just as we are. My predecessor's time as the local pastor for this local church has ended, but the work will have a new beginning.

Each ending always brings about a new beginning. How you handle it will depend on how you view it.

EXALTING THE LORD JESUS CHRIST

Bishop Lesmon R. Graham

Bishop Lesmon Graham was born in Jamaica. He attended Kingston Technical High School and worked at the University of West Indies, Mona Campus, Jamaica. He came to the United Kingdom in 1960, and worked at King Edward School, Edgbaston, and Birmingham University until 1968.

Lesmon is married to Viola. He has been associated with the Church of God of Prophecy for several years, and felt the call of God to the ministry at an early age. He has held many positions at a local level of the churches he attended, both in Jamaica and the United Kingdom.

In May 1965, the Church of God of Prophecy ordained him a licensed minister. His first pastorate was in 1966, for the Mansfield Road Church in Birmingham. In November 1968 he became pastor for the Tubbs Road Church in Harlesden, London. In July 1976, Lesmon and his family moved to Jamaica where he served as a pastor, Parish Overseer, Mission Representative for the Caribbean Islands, and National Overseer. In 1992 Lesmon Graham returned to England to become the National Overseer for the churches in the United Kingdom and France.

KEY SCRIPTURE: JOHN 3:14, 15

One of my earliest recollections of the need for all creation to give worshipful praises to God was through the words of the chorus:

Birds in the tree top singing their song
Flowers in the garden bowing down their heads

Angels are singing praises unto the Lord
Why should I not praise the Lord.

Yes, our Lord and Saviour deserves adoration from everyone who breathes the breath of life. It is regrettable that there are some who do not see the necessity or the importance of such worship and praise to God. The evil one Satan has deceived and is still deceiving humanity, by attracting man's attention to himself and other created things away from God. In Romans 1:25, the Apostle Paul shows that men took delight to 'change the truth of God into a lie, and worshipped the creature more than the Creator'. This desire is a direct result of the fall of man. What Satan could not achieve in heaven, he did on earth. Even today, mortal man is unable to withstand his deception. Men are giving their lives for the environment, the trees, animals, etc., etc. Yet some of these men are denying the existence of God.

It was in God's plan that His primal creation should care and protect (dress and keep) all His other creation. The abuse which takes place in the world should not be encouraged. However, until man recognizes and gives respect unto the Almighty God, all his energies spent on protecting the environment and enforcing his rights will be in vain. The scriptures teach that He 'will make all things new'. We ought now to be giving great attention to recognizing and pleasing God.

Jesus, in His discourse with Nicodemus, states what is required of believers: 'Ye must be born again' (John 3:7). The new quality of life cannot be obtained without Jesus Christ. 'And as Moses lifted up the serpent in the wilderness, even so must the Son of man be lifted up, that whosoever believeth in Him should not perish but have eternal life' (John 3:14, 15). Again He says: 'And I, if I be lifted up from the earth, will draw all men unto me' (John 12:32).

To be exalted is to be glorified, to be praised highly and to be praised enthusiastically. The Christian life is lived only to exalt Christ. Everyone should see and know that Christ controls and influences his life at all times. Every area of the

Christian life is lived to honour God. The love and esteem that the Christian has for Christ is reflected in the behaviour and attitude he shows to those with whom he interacts: family, friends, enemies, strangers, colleagues, and the Christian community will know how highly He is exalted by the lives we live.

God's primary plan is to save man from the bondage of sin and death. It is for this purpose that Jesus Christ was sent to the world (John 3:16). All the other blessings, which He has freely given in abundance, are secondary benefits. The tendency is for us to exert great efforts to obtain the secondary benefits and to give less attention to the primary plan of God. 'A man's life does not consist in the abundance of his possessions' (Luke 12:18). Anything that would diminish our admiration of the goodness of God is evil. Nothing must come between our Creator and us. The gods of money, intellect, material increase and fame have caused many to ignore the true God who creates all things. He creates those things and those persons whom we have made into gods. Jesus told the people of His day 'you cannot serve God and mammon'. Jesus said: 'You will love the one and hate the other' (Matthew 6:24). Man's loyalty must be to Him who is Lord and Saviour.

The Church is called by her Lord to exalt His name in all the earth. The expressions of joy and thankfulness should be the hallmark of our worship. On one occasion Jesus healed two blind men and said to them 'see that no man know it'. However the scripture says that as they went from Him, they 'spread abroad His fame in all the country' (Matthew 9:30, 31). Jesus' apostles were totally sold out to Him. His life in them affected the communities in such a way that it was said they 'turned the city upside down'. Peter and John healed a lame man at the gate of the temple; this miracle caused much rejoicing and astonishment to the people, and it was known by the entire city. We also must come to know God as the potent force who will do miracles and wonders among us. When praises are given to God from a true heart and with sincerity of spirit, He will respond with the miraculous.

Sincere worship is not done intermittently, it is a way of life. Worship is done by the Christian every minute he/she lives. 'For me to live is Christ' (Philippians 1:21; Galatians 2:20). The life of Jesus is lived by the believer with Him and others in mind. Christianity is not about being religious and doing the right things. It produces a radical change in lifestyle and outlook — a life conformed to that of the author of faith, and an outlook which is not akin to this world. When this transformation has taken place in a person, he/she does not always have the approval and the applause of others. However, this is the life to which Jesus has called us.

This world needs to see Jesus. They will see Him by the love and care given to the poor, the afflicted and the neglected, by His people (Matthew 25:34; James 1:27). The rich and poor, the old and the young, every class, culture, or status should see the Lord Jesus Christ through our lives. The message He gave is a message of hope and love. There are many hopeless people round and about us and they ought to see His love expressed through us, His Church. The Church of God is the Church of love. The Church of love must be seen to have a loving concern for a world ravaged by the evil one. The life of Christ should be seen in all our endeavours in order to challenge others to find Him. As God's children live and give witness of Christ, He will attract men to Himself. He has said 'I will draw all men unto me'.

In preparing the disciples for His departure, Jesus gave them the promise of the Comforter, the Holy Spirit, who along with His many other duties would proclaim His divinity and authority. In John 14:26, we read: 'But the Comforter, which is the Holy Spirit, whom the Father will send in my name, he shall teach you all things, and bring all things to your remembrance, whatsoever I have said unto you.' Note the term 'whatsoever I have said unto you'. The Holy Spirit bears witness to the message of Jesus Christ to this world. In John 15:26, we see where it is said of the Holy Spirit 'He shall testify of me'. Again in John 16:14: 'He shall glorify me'.

The scriptures tell us that: 'God hath highly exalted him

and given him a name which is above every name; that at the name of Jesus every knee shall bow, of things in heaven and things under the heaven, and that every tongue shall confess that Jesus Christ is Lord to the glory of God the Father' (Philippians 2:9–11).

Since God, the Father, the Holy Spirit, has glorified Him as Lord and Saviour, it is our duty to magnify Him for the salvation and victory He has brought to our lives.

ARISE AND BUILD

Reverend Kate Coleman

Kate Coleman is a Baptist minister in central London and is committed to inner-city outreach. In addition to her pastoral responsibilities Kate lectures occasionally at a number of training institutions. She also leads seminars and preaches throughout Britain and overseas on issues as diverse as spiritual welfare and the black presence in the Bible. She is also a valued member of a number of steering groups and councils of reference. Kate's concerns also include black theology and she is currently working on her PhD at the University of Birmingham.

KEY SCRIPTURES: ISAIAH 61:4; NEHEMIAH 2:20

The words of the prophet Isaiah resound with hope as we as people of God face the task that God, by His Spirit, has set before us in these days. The prophet pronounces 'They will rebuild the ancient ruins and restore the places long devastated; they will renew the ruined cities that have been devastated for generations' (Isaiah 61:4 NIV). Because so much of what we see around us in our personal lives, our communities, our nation is tinged with a sense of work that needs to be done; with a sense of changes that need to take place; these words from Isaiah are inspirational.

What am I saying today?

I am saying that the people of God have one responsibility in these days. That is to be engaged with God and to be engaging with all that God is engaged in. As we follow Jesus we discover that we have been called to the task of restoration; to the task of rebuilding, to the task of putting right what has gone wrong; to the task of seeing individuals and communities restored. But how can we be God's answer to the world today? How can we be a part of God's solution and avoid simply being part of the world's problem?

Back in Jerusalem around 450 BC Nehemiah spoke these words to his Jewish brothers and sisters: 'Come let us arise and build' (Nehemiah 2:20). The hope pronounced by the prophet Isaiah became their hope, and the events in the book of Nehemiah demonstrate that this hope did not disappoint them. Many who have followed Nehemiah have subsequently found the courage to 'arise and build'.

Nehemiah 1:2–3; 4:6–7, 13; 6:15: these few verses give us an overall sense of what some of these principles are. Allow me to set the scene for you.

Here in the book of Nehemiah we have moved from the events surrounding the first great Exodus of the Children of Israel from Egypt to the 'Promised Land' to the events surrounding the end of the last great Old Testament Exodus. This time the movement is from Babylon, but again it is to the same place of the promise.

In other words, we meet the people of God back in the place of slavery. Not Egyptian slavery this time but Babylonian slavery; slavery by another name! We meet them back in the place of bondage, back in a place of trouble. As a result of their slavery the place of God's promise to them lies in ruins and in utter devastation. They had enjoyed it for a while, they had known that blessing for a short time but somehow and some way they had lost it.

Praise God that we see clearly in scripture time and time again that God is not just the God of the first chance. He is also the God of the seventy-seventh! In many ways the book of Nehemiah is a book about second chances. After all you cannot rebuild what was not already built! And you cannot renew what was not once new! And the encouragement of this book is that God will stand with those who seek to flow in the hope expressed by the prophet Isaiah. How then do we rebuild?

1. Nehemiah's story begins with a concern

Here is someone locked in slavery and servitude in a foreign land, in exile, and yet his thoughts are not for himself, nor for his personal condition. Instead, his thoughts are for his people; these people that God loves, not simply because they are 'the people of God' but because they are *his* people; people he identifies with culturally and historically; people who are a part of him. Sometimes I hear people speaking with fear as if identifying with a particular people-group is wrong or sinful; as if it is equal to prejudice or racism; as if to be for one group necessarily means to be against another. Jesus fully identified with a fallen humanity to the point of incarnation, but we do not accuse Him of such isms against nature or the animal kingdom! The focus here is not racism or destructive nationalism or ethnocentrism. Nehemiah was concerned for the *well-being of his* people. Are you? His concern is simply for whether or not they are going along OK.

Nehemiah 1:2: ' . . . one of my brothers came from Judah with some other men and I questioned them about the Jewish remnant that survived the exile and also about Jerusalem.' When he hears the bad news about their condition he breaks down: 'When I heard these things I sat down and wept. For some days I mourned and fasted and prayed' (Nehemiah 1:4).

A man drenched in tears, not out of concern for himself but for his people. How often do you weep over the condition of God's Church? Weep, not of anger or frustration, not because someone has hurt you or irritated you, but weep because private enterprise, private empires and personal interest motivate us, it seems, more than a vision for building God's kingdom? I mean, have we ever wept simply because . . . we have failed to take our proper place within the purposes of God? Or wept simply because . . . of an all-too-common indifference to issues of righteousness and justice inside and outside the Church? Wept simply because 'hypocrisy' rather than 'integrity' is the word so linked with Christians by those outside the Church. When was the last time *you* wept, like Jesus did, over the condition of your own

113

people? And even perhaps over the condition of your own heart?

Nehemiah WEPT, we are told. He wept and he mourned, but his tears were not the tears of despair and hopelessness. These were not the tears of spiritual and physical inactivity because we are told that he 'fasted and prayed to the God of heaven' (Nehemiah 1:4). But just look at how he prayed. Not 'Lord, destroy *those* people who have destroyed Jerusalem', not 'Lord forgive my people because *they* have sinned' but '*I* confess the sins we Israelites *including myself* and my father's house have committed against you' (Nehemiah 1:6b).

But, perhaps you want to protest along with me 'hey, Nehemiah isn't to blame! After all, he's in the place of exile. He was carried off against his will. He isn't personally responsible, surely, for what is taking place in Jerusalem. He didn't torch the gates or break down the walls himself.' Yet he totally identifies with the sins that he acknowledges his own people have been guilty of committing, all the sins that have led up to the current state of affairs.

You know, we can't always absolve ourselves from blame over the state of the Church or of our people conveniently. We can't simply distance ourselves from the very real problems that our communities suffer from. Like Adam we cannot just point the finger accusingly at Eve, and like Eve we cannot simply blame the serpent for the state of affairs, because sin is not just about the things we do wrong, i.e. our sins of 'commission'. It is also about those things that we neglect to do, i.e. our sins of omission. Nehemiah recognizes that one manifestation of his own sin and that of his own people is the sin of neglect and inactivity. As far as we can tell, this is the first occasion that Nehemiah has even attempted to take steps to affect the situation.

Martin Luther King Jr wrote that 'Individuals have not started living until they can rise above the narrow confines of their individualistic concerns to the broader concerns of humanity'. Perhaps here is the turning point in Nehemiah's own heart. Have we come to the turning point in our own hearts where our concerns extend beyond our personal lives and circumstances? Have we come to the turning point in our own hearts where we are prepared to do more than just weep and mourn about surrounding circumstances? Have we come to the turning point in our own hearts where we are prepared to become agents of change?

We have good and legitimate reasons why we can't get to prayer.

Or why we can't take time to encourage others.

Or why we can't pursue justice.

But if we don't, who will? If I don't, who will? If you don't, who will?

We always *make* time for the things we think are important, like cinema, watching TV, listening to music, making phone calls and the rest of it. Perhaps the issue is not that we lack opportunity, perhaps the issue is that we lack willingness.

2. For Nehemiah, his concern became availability

We all know that God cannot resist an available person because God is seeking out the people like David who, even as the giant Goliath blocks the path of advance, still doesn't understand what the word 'impossible' really means, in the light of God. He is seeking out people who haven't been put off yet by the words 'you are unsuitable for the task'; people like Mary Seacole who hear such words but go right ahead with the call of God anyway. You see God isn't looking for skill, for wisdom or for strength.

1 Corinthians 1:27, 29 reminds us: '. . . God chose the foolish things of the world to shame the wise; God chose the weak things of this world to shame the strong. He chose the lowly things of this world and the despised things and the things that are not to nullify the things that are, so that no one may boast before him.' So, if the world insists that you are the foolish, the lowly and the despised . . . If society doesn't think much of who and what you are . . . Even if you feel useless: then you are just the sort of person God can use. You will do very nicely!

Nehemiah prayed, he waited on God, he discerned what God required of him and he took up the challenge. As he did that, various things happened to him. Firstly — he overcome his own fear.

Now it is important that you understand that I meant what I said. Nehemiah did not *lose* his fear, he *overcame* it. If we are human, we will feel the full force of fear from time to time, but to feel the *presence* of fear is not the same as feeling the *power* of fear. Fear can be felt and overcome, and God gives us the grace for it. '. . . I was very much afraid, but I said to the king . . . ' (Nehemiah 2:2b–3). He did it anyway! It could have cost him his head to be downcast in the king's presence, yet he still stepped out. We see a similar incident in the book of Ezra, a few chapters earlier (Ezra 3:3): 'Despite their fear of the people around them they [the Jews] built the altar on its foundation and sacrificed burnt offerings on it to the Lord.' When the cause of God is strong in us, even fear can be overcome. So often we think that the opposite to fear is denial or some form of superhuman courage, but these people, like Nehemiah, acted on the strength of their conviction that God was directing and leading them and they did so with a *whole* heart!

Secondly, Nehemiah developed boldness. The king asks him what it is that he wants. Nehemiah begins by expressing his desire to go home but no sooner does he have the king's consent than he gains the confidence to add a number of further requests:

For letters; for wood; for safe conduct.

As we seek to serve God's purposes we need to be bold in seeking out his provision to fulfil his purposes. It is often said that 'Where God guides, God provides'. But so many of us have never found out if it is true or not, because we have not dared to ask God for anything; not for strength, not for skill, not for wisdom, not for grace and not for finance. Yet we are still surprised when we discover that we have neither strength, skill, wisdom, grace or finance! It is God's to provide. Ours is to ask!

Finally, God granted him success, for when God's hand is

on something he knows how to make a way for it. Nehemiah said 'God's hand was on me. The king granted my requests' (Nehemiah 1:8). But 'success' does *not* mean being trouble-free because wherever God opens a door . . .

3. There is always opposition

There are a limited number of things that we can guarantee in this life. 'In this world', Jesus said, 'you will have trouble', and trouble arrives in all shapes and sizes. It is important that we understand that the experience of opposition is NOT the same as a closed door. Some of us are passively giving way to opposition when we need to resist it. On the other hand, many of us try to push open a closed door without success, a door that God has closed.

It takes discernment to tell the difference. A closed door cannot be opened even by prayer, but opposition can always be overcome. 'When Sanballat the Horonite and Tobiah the Ammonite official heard about this they were very much disturbed that someone had come to promote the welfare of the Israelites' (Nehemiah 2:10). It always amazes me when I read this verse. You'd think that other people would be pleased that someone somewhere has taken an interest in promoting the welfare of their own people, but instead we find that the reality is that they feel threatened, resentful and are sometimes even openly hostile! Sounds familiar to me!

External opposition in this instance comes from Sanballat and Tobiah (Nehemiah 6:1–4) and is, thankfully, fairly easy to identify and to counteract. By far the worst kind of opposition in the process of restoration is the opposition that comes from within the community; after all, some of the most significant and influential individuals in modern history such as Martin Luther King Jr and Malcolm X found that the fiercest and often most fatal opposition has come from within their own communities. Nehemiah experiences three forms of internal opposition.

Firstly, opposition comes from those who are simply not

interested in doing any of the actual work. We read: 'The next section was repaired by the men of Tekoa, but their nobles would not put their shoulders to the work under their supervisors' (Nehemiah 3:5). Now these are the kind of people who are very happy to live in the house that you build! Inspiration and perspiration are not part of their vocabulary! Too often I have met people who have enjoyed the labours of those who have fought for civil rights, for women's rights, or those who have struggled for liberty in so many places and yet have personally refused to take part in *any* struggle that will benefit the next generation who, after all, have to live in the houses that we build or, as the case may be, do not build effectively.

The image of war behind it may be unhelpful, but surely Winston Churchill had a point when he said during the Second World War years 'Never . . . has so much been owed by so many to so few'. It is unfortunate that churches and communities often operate in the same way. These people aid the opposition simply because they do nothing!

Secondly, opposition comes in the form of the scare-mongers. We meet them in Nehemiah 4:10–11:

Meanwhile the people in Judah said 'The strength of the labourers is giving out and there is so much rubble that we cannot rebuilt the wall'. Also our enemies said 'Before they know it or see us, we will be right among them and will kill them and put an end to the work'. The Jews who lived near them came and told us ten times over 'wherever you turn, they will attack us'.

Ten times they came! What for? It is not like Nehemiah and his co-workers were unaware of the external opposition. The scaremongers are like the people in the church and community who have the ministry of bad news. You may acquire a new car and they'll be the ones telling you why it will only last for two weeks; you'll share your vision and they will be the ones telling you why it can't work. These

118

people are only able to criticize destructively! Who needs enemies when you've got friends like these?

The third kind of internal opposition comes from those who are supposed to be working with you but who are allowing the enemy to work through them. 'Also in those days the nobles of Judah were sending to Tobiah and replies from Tobiah kept coming to them' (Nehemiah 6:17). And if opposition in the work is inevitable, then vigilance is a necessity: 'Therefore I stationed some of the people behind the lowest points of the wall at the exposed places, posting them by families with their swords, spears and bows' (Nehemiah 4:13).

Perhaps one of the most important things to note is . . .

4. In the rebuilding process everyone has their part to play

Nehemiah may have been the catalyst just as Martin Luther King Jr, Olaudah Equiano and Harriet Tubman were catalysts in the process, but in the end, they weren't sole players. They never operated entirely alone. Without the support of others nothing is possible. Someone once said that the definition of success is to 'find some like-minded people and stick with them'. Neither could Nehemiah have accomplished as much as he was able to do in such a short space of time without the help of others around him.

Nehemiah 3:1: 'Eliashib the High Priest and his fellow priests went to work and rebuilt the sheep gate.'

Nehemiah 3:12: 'Shallum son of Hallohesh, ruler of a half district of Jerusalem, repaired the next section with the help of his daughters.'

Nehemiah 3:17: 'Next to him, the repairs were made by the Levites under Rehum son of Bani.'

Men and women, priests and merchants, Levites and rulers. Everyone has their part to play and as each one sets their hearts fully to the task at hand they are able to achieve a great deal in an incredibly short period of time. We are told that, surprisingly, the wall was rebuilt in 52 days (Nehemiah 6:15)! We can be encouraged and strengthened in the tasks that we face both because of the presence of others, whether they be friends, family, church or community members, i.e. those who stand around us right now and put their hands to the work; but we can also be encouraged by the examples and experiences of those who have gone before us.

In Nehemiah 3:16 we read the following: 'Beyond him, Nehemiah son of Azbuk, ruler of a half district of Beth Zur, made repairs up to a point opposite the tombs of David as far as the artificial pool and the House of Heroes.'

5. In any community the 'House of Heroes' becomes a focal point

As Christians we take our inspiration from Jesus and other biblical characters of faith such as Deborah, Moses, Zelophehad's daughters, Joseph, Priscilla and Paul. These heroes and heroines are those who have paved the way; they are those who accomplished much. In turn, they become those who inspire us to move on.

In Ghana, where I was born, we have a symbol for the phrase *Sankofa*. The symbol means learning and wisdom from the past and it is an encouragement to return to 'pick up' or to learn from the past. Perhaps Nehemiah gained strength and encouragement from others who had shown the same concern as he had and who preceded him; others such as Zerubbabel who worked alongside the prophet Haggai, or Ezra alongside the prophet Zechariah.

My own house of heroes includes people like Mary Prince who published her autobiography in 1831 to aid the abolitionist cause; Olaudah Equiano, a Nigerian Christian who sought the welfare of black people in eighteenth-century Britain. In addition, Sojourner Truth was spurred on by her faith in Jesus to fight both the abolitionist and women's cause in America, and of course there are countless others who have prayed, cared, persevered and resisted defeat, whose names we may never know.

Jesus is at work today, rebuilding and restoring the devastated lives of human beings. We are called to imitate this Jesus in his work by becoming involved in the repair of lives and communities, praying, taking action and paving a way that others can follow. Is it not, therefore, time for us as women and men of faith to 'arise and build'?

THE SPIRIT OF LIFE

Reverend Paul Morson

Reverend Paul Morson lives in the Birmingham area of England. He originated from the British West Indies island of Montserrat (the island with the recent volcanic problem). He came to England as a teenager in 1960, and has lived in the Birmingham area ever since. Paul has been married twice. His first wife died in 1979, leaving him two children, Tracey and Lisa. His current wife is Monica, whom he married in 1989.

The God of love, grace, mercy and truth graciously saved him in 1965, and has kept him by His grace ever since.

He attends the Assemblies of the First Born, whose General Headquarters is St Stephen's Church, Battersea Bridge Road, London SW11. The Assemblies of the First Born is a black-led Pentecostal movement, and has about twenty churches throughout England.

Paul also works as an authorized minister within the Asbury Circuit of the Methodist Church in Birmingham. This consists of eight churches within the areas of Lozells, Handsworth, Perry Barr, Great Barr and Pheasey.

As a minister, Paul's primary aim is to glorify God and edify all His people, and he has pledged to give unconditional support to any individual or group who advocate similar aims.

KEY SCRIPTURE: ROMANS 8:2

For the law of the Spirit of life in Christ Jesus hath made me free from the law of sin and death.

In this sermon I will be expounding the doctrinal reality of life in the Holy Spirit of Life. My primary aim is to give assurance to those who have the Spirit of life in Christ Jesus, and to awaken those who don't have Him, bearing in mind that scripture emphatically states in Romans 8:9 'That if any man have not the Spirit of Christ, he is none of His'. For us to live a born-again life, the Holy Spirit must live in us. When He is living in us he brings to us what Christ the great high priest; the anointed one; the great shepherd of the flock has purchased for us on Calvary's tree. He assures us of sins forgiven, and gives us grace to live lives that please God.

Because of this fact, we can say with assurance that we have been saved from sin and have received eternal life through the merits of the eternal Christ. The source of this new life is God the eternal Father. The applier of this new life is the eternal Spirit. The evidence of this new life is our personal awareness of the indwelling presence of the Godhead within us.

According to the teaching of Christ in John 14:23, He himself and God the Father takes up residence within each born-again saint, and according to Paul's teaching in Romans 8:9, the blessed Holy Spirit dwells within all born-again saints.

When this transaction has taken place, the Godhead imparts a new nature within, which is compatible with divine nature. Because of the impartation of this divine nature, the Holy Spirit within us can cause the written word of scripture to become the living or incarnate Word of Life. We then in turn can cause the written word to become the living word through the spoken word, through the Spirit that dwells in us. In order for us to extract the life of Christ from the scripture, the blessed Holy Spirit must make a number of applications or manifestation in our lives. And it is of paramount importance that we grasp the process and purpose of these manifestations, for if we go wrong here, we will go wrong in every other aspect of our salvation. The word of Christ in John 16:8 teaches us that 'When the Holy Spirit is come, he will reprove the world of sin [what we are and what we have committed], of righteousness [what God

123

requires from us], and judgement [what we will receive if we don't measure up to God's standard of righteousness]'.

The word 'reprove' in this context means to blame, to reprimand, and to condemn. And the primary purpose of ascertaining blame, or to reprimand or to condemn, is to produce conviction within the individual.

Therefore, the first application of the Holy Spirit in the life of the unsaved person is in the form of the *convicting Spirit*. He convinces and convicts us of the sinner we are and the sins we have committed. This process is very important for mankind, especially those who are in the upper social class, and those who have been brought up in the environment of the Church. Most of these people may accept moral mistakes, but refuse to acknowledge themselves as sinners. The convicting Spirit must show these people, together with all unregenerate hearts, that their very nature is sinful, and because of this fact, all their thoughts and practices, although justified by society and even the Church, appear in the sight of God as evil continually.

Something must be done to change both the nature and attitude of the individual, and the convicting work of the Spirit of Life is the only remedy provided by, and acceptable unto God.

In Palestine there are two symbolic mountains: Mount Sinai and Mount Calvary. Mount Sinai proclaims judgement and declares that the wages of sin is death. Mount Calvary proclaims mercy and declares that the gift of God is eternal life through Jesus Christ our Lord.

At conviction, the Holy Spirit will point mankind to both Sinai and Calvary. His response to Sinai must be one of fright, as a convicted man who has any kind of remorse is always a frightened man. Therefore, when the Holy Spirit points us to Sinai, our emotional response should be one of fear. Fear of death, fear of God's impending judgement, fear of hell, fear of eternal separation from the God of love.

On the other hand, the same convicting Spirit will also point us to the only God-ordained remedy for sinners and their sins — Mount Calvary. There we can behold the Lamb of God who taketh away the sins of the world, including yours and mine. There on Calvary we can see for ourselves Christ dying in our place. There we can see him being wounded for our transgressions, and being bruised for our iniquities.

If we respond positively to the wooing of the Holy Spirit, and accept God's one and only gift of salvation, then God the Father will pour out his love upon us and within us. And together with the Father and the Son, the blessed Holy Spirit will take up his abode in us, and we will then become the temple of the living Godhead, and heirs to eternal life.

This is not a one-off experience, for the same convicting Spirit stays with us throughout our lifetime, working on our consciences, giving us the ability to assess and evaluate the things which are pleasing to the Godhead, and the things which are not.

The next application of the blessed Holy Spirit in the life of a convicted sinner is the *indwelling Spirit*. It is erroneously practised, and even taught in some Church circles, that the Holy Spirit is a force that takes over certain individuals within a given service in order to enhance their emotional performances. This is contrary to the doctrinal teaching of scripture, which presents the Blessed Holy Spirit as a person. He is co-equal with the Father and the Son. He is co-eternal with the Father and the Son. Therefore, to consider him as a force is to devalue his divinity.

Jesus' teaching in John 14:16–17 affirms that the Blessed Holy Spirit is a person. And He equates and relates Him to Himself and the Father. His teaching in this particular scripture, states that 'He will pray the Father, and He shall send you another Comforter [an advocate equal to Himself], that He may abide with you forever [eternally]'. The pronoun 'He', in this context, represents a person and not a force. 'Jesus', this person in verse 17, is the Spirit of Truth whom (representing a person) the world cannot receive. The reason why the world cannot receive the life-giving Spirit is because they have not been convicted of sin and of righteousness and of judgement. They have not responded positively to God's only remedy for their sins.

Therefore, in their unconvicted state, they cannot receive the indwelling Spirit while their hearts and minds are shut to Calvary and Sinai. But those who positively respond to the merciful wooing of the Spirit of Life, and repent of their sins, are in effect opening up their hearts and minds to receive the blessed indwelling Spirit. And together with the Father and the Son, the Blessed Holy Spirit takes up his abode in their spirit as the indwelling Spirit.

From the moment we receive the indwelling Spirit into our spirit, he starts immediately and constantly to bear witness with our spirit that we are the children of God. And he gives us the right to address the Almighty God, the God of all creation, as our own Father, thus establishing both an active and positive relationship between humanity and divinity. From then on, we become aware of God's abiding presence, and have the ability to recognize his voice.

Verse 14 of the same chapter in Romans assures us that 'As many as are led by the indwelling Spirit of God, they are His sons and daughters'. Verse 9 also warns us that 'if any man or woman have not the Spirit of Christ, they are none of His'.

It is possible for us as members of Christ's Church, who have the indwelling Spirit abiding in us, to quench Him. When the indwelling Spirit is quenched within us, we lose all sense of God's Holy presence and the ability to discern His voice. But that does not mean that the indwelling Spirit is not present within us. Only that we have lost the awareness of Him. When this happens, the convicting Spirit will immediately start to work on our conscience, encouraging us to repent of the sin which caused the quenching, in order to restore our awareness of His indwelling presence.

It is entirely up to us to remain responsive to the leading of the indwelling Spirit, and that our relationship and fellowship with Him remain constant. This verse of scripture from Romans 8:11 should be part of our daily meditation. It reads thus: 'But if the Spirit of him that raised Christ from the dead dwell in you, he that raised up Christ from the dead shall also quicken (bring to life) your mortal bodies by *his Spirit that dwelleth in you.*'

Another manifestation of the Holy Spirit in the life of the believer is the *transforming Spirit*. Because of our sinful nature, radical changes within us are of paramount importance in order for the Godhead to constantly dwell within us. The convicting Spirit shows us that we have this innate iniquitous nature of gross wickedness and injustice. All our attitudes, all our desires, all our behaviours are generated and motivated from this unregenerate sinful nature. Therefore, in order for us to have the life of the Spirit of Christ within us, a transformation must take place within our spirit by the Spirit of Life. Any work of the flesh has its source in our spirit. Therefore, the transforming Spirit must first transform our spirit, which will in turn result in the cleansing of our flesh.

Our spiritual parts which consist of our mind — the seat of intellect; our heart — the seat of emotion; our conscience — the seat of evaluation; our soul and spirit — the seat of desires and purpose: all these spiritual organs need to be cleansed by the blood of Christ, and transformed into His likeness. The reason why this transformation is of paramount importance is that every relationship between the Godhead and us is made through these organs. Through these organs the scripture becomes alive in our everyday experiences. Through them, His word can penetrate our very being, enabling us to be aware of God's presence in our lives.

In Psalm 51, we learn that when King David committed the physical sin of adultery with Bathsheba, he was more concerned about the life of his spiritual being than that of his physical being. His cry of repentance regarding his spiritual organs is heard in verses 6 and 10. Let us now listen to him, and if necessary, cry with him: 'Behold, thou desirest truth in the inward parts [mind, heart, conscience, soul and spirit]: and in the hidden part thou shalt make me to know wisdom . . . Create in me a clean heart [the convicting Spirit convicts him of the urgent need for inward cleansing]; and renew a right spirit within me.' He recognized that while his heart was defiled, his spirit couldn't be right.

In verse 11, we learn the importance of our awareness of

God's divine presence, and the danger of losing such awareness when we sin. David's repentance includes a godly sorrow for his sin; a verbal confession; a turning away from sin; an acceptance of God's forgiveness for his sin; restoration to the joy of God's salvation; and a willingness to testify to others about the grace and mercy of God.

The transforming Spirit is not only involved in dealing with our humanity; He will also be involved in dealing with our eternal change. It is the same transforming Spirit who is now within us, together with the indwelling Spirit who will hear the voice of the trumpet, and change our vile bodies, that we may be fashioned like unto His glorious body.

Our final expounding of the Spirit of Life is His manifestation as the *empowering Spirit*. Knowledge, be it sacred or secular, is power. Jesus states in John 8:31–32 that: 'If ye continue in my word, then are ye my disciples indeed; and ye shall know the truth, and the truth shall make you free.' Only the empowering Spirit can give us knowledge of the truth, and this takes place when the written word becomes the living or incarnate word, through the power of the life-giving Spirit within a believer. Only the empowering Spirit within us can enable us to know the truth.

Knowing the truth is to know the God of truth; the Word of truth; the Spirit of truth; the Christ of truth; and the Church, which is the ground and pillar of truth. These are areas of truth, which are of vital importance for the health of a Christian. In John 16:13, Jesus teaches us that: 'When the Spirit of truth is come [to dwell within us], he will guide us into all [areas of] truth.' Therefore, in order for us to know the areas of truth mentioned in John 8:32, the empowering Spirit has to guide us into those areas of truth.

If we miss our mark here, then the truth for us becomes nothing more than the idea and ideals of traditional religious leaders, something used by them to justify their assumed positions, which they use to control, exploit and manipulate their followers. In John 14:6, Jesus said that He is the way, the truth and the life. And He continues to emphasize that no one cometh unto the Father but by Him.

Jesus is implying that the knowledge of truth must start with Him. For He is not only truth, but also the source of such truth. In verse 7, He exposed Thomas's ignorance of Him. He told Thomas that if he had known Him (Jesus), then he should have known the Father also. For He is the only way that leads to the Father. He is the only truth that is of the Father. He is the only life that is given by the Father. It is the task of the Spirit of truth to empower us with the knowledge of these divine truths, which are effectively hid from the wise and the prudent of this world.

In Jesus' high priestly prayer, recorded in John 17, He proclaimed that eternal life is to *know the only true God, and Jesus whom He has sent.* The empowering Spirit imparts to us such knowledge. And together with the indwelling Spirit, gives us the assurance of eternal life.

In conclusion, I am convinced that human personality is made for divine indwelling. And until the Godhead takes up abode in mankind, that mankind is incomplete. I also affirm and declare that if any individual has been through these processes, especially that of the convicting and indwelling Spirit, then they can say with all faith and assurance, that 'Christ is in me, the hope of glory. And in the same Christ dwelleth all the fullness of God bodily. Therefore, the Spirit of life hath made me free from the law of sin and death, and has imparted to me the life of the risen Christ.'

On the other hand, if anyone has not been through these processes, and has never been consciously aware of the convicting and indwelling Spirit, then it is time to consider your ways, and equate and relate what you term salvation, with that of the life of the Spirit of Christ.

We will now conclude our sermon with a prayer of intercession:

Almighty and ever-living Father, we thank You for Your Holy word of truth. May it be a lamp unto our feet, a light unto our path, and strength to our lives. Take us and use us to love and to serve in the power of the Holy Spirit and in the Holy name of Your Son and our Saviour Jesus Christ our Lord.

You have given us grace at this time, with one accord, to make our common supplication to You. And You have promised that where two or three are gathered in Your name, You will grant their request. Fulfil now, O Lord, the desires and petitions of your servants. Grant us in this world knowledge of your love, and in the world to come, life everlasting.

And now may the love of our Lord and Saviour Jesus Christ draw us to Himself. May the power of our Lord and Saviour Jesus Christ strengthen us in this life. May the Spirit of our Lord and Saviour Jesus Christ fill our hearts with his love, and may His grace bless our future and give us the assurance of life in His eternal presence, and may his blessings be with us and remain with us, now and always. Amen!

BRINGING A NIGHTMARE TO AN END

Pastor Hughes Redhead

Hughes Redhead was born on 9 September 1952 in Grenada in the Caribbean, and arrived in England at the age of 9. He is married to Patricia and has three children: Luke, Marcus and Rebecca.

Hughes accepted Jesus when he was about 6, and preached a very short sermon to his great-grandmother, who was a Roman Catholic, at about 7. Hughes asked her to accept Jesus so that she would not die and go to hell. She chased him out of the house.

Hughes was baptized in water at 15, and baptized with the Holy Spirit about a year later. He served in various ministries at the local church in which he grew up. He also served as a regional youth leader and as a regional and national evangelist.

He is currently pastoring The Hope of Rotherham. Hughes' personal vision is to be a role model for at least one person of someone who loves and serves God.

KEY SCRIPTURE: HEBREWS 2:14–15

Our dreams

We all have dreams. Most of them we are not able to remember. There are times when you have a dream that is so good you are disappointed to wake up and find that it was only a dream. You are annoyed with whoever might have woken you. Other dreams are the very opposite; we call them nightmares.

One common nightmare is where you find yourself falling from a great height. You shout for help but no one hears. You continue to fall. There is no net to land in, nothing like the branch of a tree to grab on to, to break your fall. You save yourself only by waking up.

Another common nightmare is where someone or something frightens you. You try to get away from them, but no matter how fast or how far you run they reappear before you, forcing you to run in another direction. Even after waking from such a dream you are still afraid. You lie very still hoping that whatever is in the dark is unaware of the sweat on your brow and the pounding of your heart.

My nightmares

Children have their fair share of nightmares. When I was about 6 years of age I had a dream in which I was standing with a great crowd of people in a large plain. We were all dressed in white gowns. Suddenly everyone left the earth and was going up into the sky; in what I knew was the rapture. Jesus had returned and everyone was going up. Well, everyone except me, I was being left behind. As my mum went up I grabbed onto her feet, but it was a long way up and I got tired and had to let go. I fell. I was awake before I hit the ground. After that dream, I realized that I could no longer rely on my mum to carry me; I had to hold on to Jesus myself. Better still, to let Him hold on to me.

On 10 March 1997, Patricia and I celebrated our eighteenth wedding anniversary. My worst nightmare as an adult took place when we were courting. I dreamt that I had married someone else. It was someone I knew but had no romantic interest in her. After the wedding I suddenly thought about Patricia, 'I can't marry her now'. Then I thought about my new bride and how I might get rid of her. (Remember, I'm only dreaming.) 'I can't kill her, that would be wrong. I can't divorce her to get married again, that would also be wrong.' Then I started wondering how I got myself into such a mess. I woke up in a cold sweat, glad to find myself still single.

The blind man at Jericho

Real life can sometimes turn into a bad dream. The Bible tells us about a man whose life can easily be described as a nightmare: in Luke 18:35–37 we read: 'As Jesus approached Jericho, a blind man was sitting by the roadside begging. When he heard the crowd going by, he asked what was happening. They told him, "Jesus of Nazareth is passing by".'

I want you to get a picture of this man — to see him. He was blind. He lived in the dark — one long night. He was not a blind man with a large inheritance and servants to look after him. He was poor. But he was not simply a poor man living off what he received from relatives and friends. He was a beggar who sat by the roadside begging.

When we think about the roadsides where he begged, we need to exchange horse manure for the exhaust fumes of our cars. He had to contend with dust and dirt kicked up on him as the rich and the strong rode by. He had to be led to the place to beg. He ate what he was given. If it started raining guess who was the last one to find somewhere dry? Yes, the blind beggar.

He could not see the changing seasons. He could feel the cold but could not see the crystal flakes of the snow as they settled on him and all around him. He missed the shades of green, the flowers and the rainbow in the raindrops. He was blind and he was begging.

But he had something going for him — he could hear. And as the scripture says, 'He who has ears to hear let him hear'. One day he sensed a change in the pace of the footsteps around him. Soon there was a crowd of people passing, with more joining them all the time. They were laughing, shouting, excited. He used his ears to hear.

Not only could he hear but he could speak. So he used the voice he had and asked those around him what was happening. They told him 'Jesus of Nazareth is passing by'. Suddenly he 'saw' how his nightmare could end. In his mind he was already seeing the approach of daylight. He had heard of Jesus and how he made the lame to walk, the dumb to talk,

133

he had raised the dead to life and he had opened the eyes of other blind people.

This was his chance. He opened his mouth and called out 'Jesus, Son of David, have mercy on me!' It's hard to believe this, but the people in front of him told him to be quiet. But he was the one living in unending night. He shouted even louder 'Son of David, have mercy on me!'

Jesus heard him and called him

Guess what? Jesus heard him. With the clamour from the entire crowd, with all the shouting and commotion, Jesus heard his cry for help. He stopped and ordered that the man be brought to him. The prophet Isaiah said 'How gracious He will be when you cry for help! As soon as He hears He will answer you' (Isaiah 30:19).

When Jesus called him the crowd parted, creating a path for the blind man. A path leading to Jesus. He was no longer just a blind poor beggar. He was a man whom Jesus had called, who was now the centre of attention. A man about to meet his God. Again he was given an opportunity to use what he had, his hearing and his voice, to get what he wanted, his sight. Jesus asked him 'What do you want me to do for you?'

'Lord, I want to see', he replied.

Jesus said to him 'Receive your sight, your faith has healed you'. Immediately he received his sight and followed Jesus, praising God. When all the people saw it, they also praised God.

His nightmare was over. He left the darkness and entered the light.

Today's nightmares

Like the blind man of Jesus' day we sometimes face situations in which we would like to believe that we were only dreaming, that we would wake up to find it never happened. We may face these difficulties as individuals, as families, as communities, as a nation or as a race; with one generation living through the same pain and suffering which their parents were released from only through death.

Private nightmares

Private nightmares can range from the threat of death and illness to financial loss and poverty. You don't have to lose your job to enter a financial crisis. A little over-stretched with your mortgage, a lack of discipline with credit cards, or a short-term loan with high interest rates; add to this a short period of difficulties with payments and before long you could find yourself facing repossession, your marriage in difficulties, and performance at work deteriorating.

Shared nightmares

Some nightmares affect whole communities and make the headlines: the massacre of 5- and 6-year-olds at school at Dunblane, Scotland, and the stabbing to death of the black teenager Stephen Lawrence at a bus stop by a gang of white racists, because he was black.

Most people in our communities do not face these horrors, but because of the constant reporting of bad news we do enter other people's nightmares. A number of reports following research have found that the fear of crime is often much greater than the crime levels warrant. Many elderly people are afraid to answer their own door for fear of being mugged, whilst in some areas women are virtually under curfew because of fear of attack. Reports over the past few years have suggested that the main reason why people are not moving house is because of the fear of losing their jobs. So the housing market remains depressed.

Every now and then we have a scare about our food, the latest being the human equivalent of BSE or mad cow disease. Meanwhile the constant vigil of our health authorities monitors the progress of the AIDS virus with the misery and death which follows in its wake.

Those of us who are Christians have to face the facts that

many Christians contribute to the fifty million-plus abortions worldwide every year. Nor can we escape the question of how it was that in Rwanda, one of the most Christianized countries in Africa, within a few weeks, hundreds of thousands of Tutsis were killed by their Hutu neighbours — many of them Christian neighbours.

Meanwhile in Europe, Christian Europe, fifty years after the Holocaust the Jews relive their suffering, with Swiss bankers unwilling to acknowledge that gold in their vaults belonged to victims of Nazi Germany. With many of the survivors already dead, that model of nations, under the threat of further exposures and possible sanctions, is doing too little too late to return to the Jews what their killers took from them.

Finally, we have the African Americans who have gone from slavery through lynching and segregation to crack cocaine. It should not surprise anyone that many are now abandoning the Christianity of their white tormentors and choosing Islam.

Our greatest nightmare

Yet our greatest struggle and the strongest forces which oppose us comes not from other people but from within us. The Apostle Paul puts in words the inner conflict which we all go through because of our addiction to sin: 'For what I want to do I do not do, but what I hate I do . . . It is no longer I myself that do it, but it is sin living in me . . . For I have a desire to do what is good, but I cannot carry it out . . . no, the evil that I do not want to do — this I keep on doing' (Romans 7:15–20).

Our greatest nightmares come from our rebellion against God, our Father and Creator, and from the fear which follows, the fear of death. But Jesus shared in our humanity ' . . . so that by his death he might destroy him who holds the power of death — that is the devil — and free all those who all their lives were held in slavery by their fear of death' (Hebrews 2:14–15).

Today for all who will call to him Jesus replaces the power of death with the power of His perfect love. 'There is no fear in love. But perfect love drives out fear' (1 John 4:18).

Bringing the nightmare to an end

What can anyone in any of these nightmares do? Do what the blind man did: call to Jesus for help. When the blind man called out to him, Jesus was on his way to die on the cross and bring our greatest nightmare, our separation from our God, to an end. Call on Him and He will turn your night into brightest day.

A NEW AND LIVING WAY

Reverend Carl Smith

Carl Smith is currently a National Evangelist of the Church of God of Prophecy. He has pastored three churches over a period of nine years in the London area. He has also served as National Youth Secretary and PR Director.

He is married and has three daughters and a son.

KEY SCRIPTURE: HEBREWS 10:19–23

> *Therefore, brethren, having boldness to enter the Holiest by the blood of Jesus, by a new and living way which He consecrated for us, through the veil, that is, His flesh, and having a High Priest over the house of God, let us draw near with a true heart in full assurance of faith, having our hearts sprinkled from an evil conscience and our bodies washed with pure water. Let us hold fast the confession of our hope without wavering, for He who promised is faithful.*

In the first century of the Christian era, the presentation of the Gospel to a Gentile took a different approach to that of a Jew. The book of Acts of the Apostles gives several instances of this difference. When a Gentile was dealt with on matters about his soul, he was convinced of the reality of the 'unknown God' of creation who was, above all else, the giver of all good things and who, through His creative power, was also the creator and sustainer of all life forms (Acts 14:15–17; 17:22–32).

In contrast, when an appeal was made to a Jew on matters concerning the salvation of his soul, the Gospel was presented as the fulfilment of Old Testament typology. In the book of Romans, Paul states this well when he says 'Chiefly because to them were committed the oracles of God' (3:2). This difference of approach is also due to the fact that to them 'pertain the adoption, the glory, the covenants, the giving of the law, the service of God, and the promises' (9:4).

That there was to be a change in the Mosaic economy and its divinely instituted services, to a Jewish mind indeed meant thinking the impossible. Therefore, the preparatory nature of the Mosaic economy meant that it was absolutely essential that a Jew must be convinced of the superior nature of the Gospel dispensation to the law dispensation. Moreover, he needed to experience the power of the Gospel in order to learn of the measureless superiority of the Gospel over all the forms, and rites, and provisions of the old covenant. This he needed to see by vivid comparison and contrast between the New and Old Testaments. This would bring him face to face with the unmistakable reality that the Gospel of Jesus Christ was the absolute fulfilment and perfection of the divine will.

Furthermore, a Jew had to learn that the Gospel was not a supplement to the law, nor can there be any supplement to the Gospel. There is no going beyond it, no adding to it; there is only one Gospel and one message. In this age of plurality where men are being offered alternatives, I believe many are becoming increasingly uncomfortable with the idea of a single Gospel message for all people. Hence, I believe the Gospel needs to be reaffirmed even more firmly and fully today.

The Epistle to the Hebrews, written primarily to Jewish Christians, especially to those who were tempted to return to Judaism, is concerned throughout to exhibit the superiority of the Gospel over the covenant and its services connected with Moses and the giving of the law. The author accomplished this, not by minimizing the old covenant, but by showing the perfection and finality of the new covenant established by Christ. In other words, rather than belittling Judaism, he shows how the new covenant transforms the old and honours it by finally fulfilling it.

In the book of Romans we are shown how the Gospel relates to Israel dispensationally, but in Hebrews we are shown how the Gospel fulfils the ordinances, the offerings, the priesthood and the tabernacle of the old economy. Among the books of the New Testament, the Epistle to the Hebrews occupies a unique place. For it is here that the Holy Spirit gives the most wonderful revelation of our Lord's heavenly priesthood and intercessory ministry. These two aspects of our Lord's mediatorial ministry are of great significance for believers living in the age of grace.

If we, however, are to catch the focal significance of these truths in the Epistle to the Hebrews, we must also appreciate its standpoint, namely how it corresponds with the book of Leviticus and the book of Exodus. The offerings and sacrifices enjoined and particularized in these books show in typical forms various aspects of our Lord's sacrifice. Outside of the Old Testament there is nowhere else that this is more clearly illustrated than in the Epistle to the Hebrews.

Therefore, as types give way to anti-type and shadows give way to substance, so our Lord's ministry and sacrifice became actual benefits for those who are redeemed and are in a covenanted relationship with God through His Son Jesus Christ. In other words, what the law could not do grace provided.

This new position of believers is typically illustrated in the history of Israel's redemption from Egypt. The nation of Israel being redeemed from Egypt was brought into a covenanted relationship with God at Mount Sinai. By virtue of the covenant, God took up His dwelling among them by a visible token of His presence among them. Therefore the book of Leviticus commences with the words 'Now the Lord called unto Moses, and spoke to him from the tabernacle of meeting' (1:1). The tabernacle and its attendant ministries and services were the visible sign of the old covenant relation between God and Israel. Likewise, the Epistle to the Hebrews was intended to show how already redeemed sinners are recipients and participators in the new covenant privileges. Thus, the author could confidently address his readers as 'Holy brethren, partakers of the heavenly calling, consider the Apostle and High Priest of our confession,

Christ Jesus' (3:1). Here the author expounds some of the profoundest fundamentals of the Christian faith, especially that of our Lord's heavenly priesthood. Thus the doctrinal importance occupied by this Epistle necessitates that it should be warmly received and studied by all who desire to know the fullness of the spiritual provisions freely given to us in the new covenant.

Those covenant provisions and privileges are expressed in terms of a 'better' deliverer and a 'better' covenant, established on 'better' principles. The Epistle commences, therefore, by showing Jesus as the God-man having greater honour than angels (chapters 1, 2), and as the new apostle, he is better than Moses (chapter 3); also as the new leader he is better than Joshua (4:8) and as our Great High Priest he is better than Aaron (4:14–16; 5:1–4). Hence the new covenant has better 'hope' (7:19), through better sacrifices which open up a 'better' sanctuary (9:23, 24), which produce 'better' results (10:1–18).

Therefore, faith is the better principle of response to those better things (10:22). The writer then went on to prove, from the example of men and women in the past, that faith has always been the principle by which the better things of the new covenant are received and enjoyed (chapter 11). Finally, it is expressed in endurance, perseverance (12:1, 2), and in the practical sanctity of life (13:4). Thus these virtues are better encouraged among believers when their faith is focused on a better country, a better resurrection, and finally, to inherit God's better things (11:16, 35, 40 respectively).

In the light of these better things, the finality and perfection of Christ's redemptive work and the permanent character of the new covenant are expressed by the statements, 'so Christ was offered *once* to bear the sins of many' (9:28), 'through the offering of the body of Jesus Christ *once* for all' (10:10).

Furthermore, the Epistle is punctuated with the solemn admonitions 'let us', beginning at chapter 4:

Let us fear lest any of you seem to have come short of it
. . . Let us therefore be diligent to enter that rest, lest

141

anyone fall according to the same example of disobedience
. . . Seeing then that we have a great High Priest who has
passed through the heavens, Jesus the Son of God, let us
hold fast our confession . . . Let us therefore come boldly
to the throne of grace, that we may obtain mercy and find
grace to help in time of need. (verses 1, 11, 14, 16)

Chapter 6:

Therefore, leaving the discussion of the elementary
principles of Christ, let us go on to perfection, not laying
again the foundation of repentance from dead works and
of faith toward God. (verse 1)

Chapter 10:

Let us draw near with a true heart in full assurance of
faith, having our hearts sprinkled from an evil conscience
and our bodies washed with pure water. Let us hold fast
the confession of our hope without wavering, for He who
promised is faithful. And let us consider one another in
order to stir up love and good works. (verses 22, 23, 24)

Chapter 12:

Therefore we also, since we are surrounded by so great
a cloud of witnesses, let us lay aside every weight, and the
sin which so easily ensnares us, and let us run with
endurance the race that is set before us . . . Therefore,
since we are receiving a kingdom which cannot be shaken,
let us have grace, by which we may serve God acceptably
with reverence and godly fear. (verses 1, 28)

Chapter 13:

Therefore let us go forth to Him, outside the camp,
bearing His reproach. (verse 13)
[Finally] Therefore by Him let us continually offer the
sacrifice of praise to God, that is, the fruit of our lips,
giving thanks to His name. (verse 15)

As mysterious as it might seem, God created us to have fellowship with Himself, but sin entered the world through Adam's disobedience and estranged human nature from fellowship with God. Hence, the leading thoughts of our Lord's heavenly priesthood are restoration, communion and fellowship. In contrast, therefore, between Christ and Aaron, the abrogating as well as the transcendent superiority of the Gospel economy is set over against the fading nature of the sacerdotal system of Judaism and the old covenant. This is fully expressed in the believers' position in Christ: 'For by one offering He has perfected forever those who are being sanctified' (10:14). This the writer explains by showing that Christ has obtained a better priesthood than that of Aaron, 'having become High Priest forever according to the order of Melchizedek' (6:20). Melchizedek was a priest of promise under the patriarchal dispensation. His priesthood, therefore, took on a universal character under which there was 'neither Jew nor Gentile'. Furthermore, the order of priesthood to which Melchizedek belonged was not fettered or limited by the Mosaic economy of law and ordinances. Therefore he offered up sacrifices not for a particular nation, but for the whole human race, without any distinction. On the other hand the restrictive and limited economy of law and solemn ceremonies to which the Aaronic priesthood belonged was, says Paul the Apostle, 'added because of transgressions, till the Seed should come to whom the promise was made' (Galatians 3:19).

The superior nature of this priesthood over that of the Aaronic priesthood is also verified historically in Abraham's life. The very fact that the whole official order and dignity of the Aaronic priesthood, represented by Abraham, was subordinate to the order of Melchizedek is seen in the fact that Abraham acknowledged Melchizedek as King of Salem and Priest of the most High God, and to whom he also gave a tenth part of all (Hebrews 7). This act of Abraham, to whom the promise was made, confirmed the official dignity of the Melchizedek priesthood above that of the Aaronic priesthood, which was subsequently instituted under the law.

But even more astonishingly, he who had no genealogy, nor the stated time when he commenced and ceased from his priestly functions, was a type of forerunner of the Son of God.

Under the law the High Priest commenced his official duties at 30 and ceased at 50 years of age, but the writer says that Melchizedek 'remains a priest continually' (verse 3), that is, as long as he lived Melchizedek continued in his priestly functions. The silence concerning Melchizedek's ancestry, his priestly pedigree, birth and death, serves to illustrate the eternal and changeless priesthood of Christ, 'who has come, not according to the law of a fleshly commandment, but according to the power of an endless life' (7:16).

The temporal mode of the Aaronic order is judged by the fact that being typical in nature, it made nothing perfect. In other words, the Levitical order had no power to bring men into a reconciled relationship with God, but 'the bringing in of a better hope, through which we draw near to God' (7:19). Hence the change of priesthood, 'For on the one hand there is an annulling of the former commandment [in which the Aaronic priesthood consists] because of its weakness and unprofitableness' (7:18). In other words, if perfection were obtainable through the Levitical order, then there would be no further need that another priest should rise after the order of Melchizedek.

Chapter 6:16 reads: 'For men indeed swear by the greater, and an oath for confirmation is for them an end of all dispute.' Here we are told that an oath is the highest kind of assurance that can be given by one man to another concerning the truth of his declarations and the sincerity of his intentions. Therefore, the writer says: 'For when God made a promise to Abraham, because He could swear by no one greater, He swore by Himself, saying, Surely blessing I will bless you, and multiplying I will multiply you' (verses 13, 14).

That is, in order to guarantee to Abraham and subsequent generations the most satisfactory evidence of the certainty of the fulfilment of the promise of future blessings, God confirmed it by an oath, and since there is none greater than Himself, nor any third party to whom he could appeal, nor any to whom he is answerable for the performance of the oath, God appealed to the absolute perfection of His own being and eternal attributes, and pledged them as a guarantee of His faithfulness and the absolute certainty of the performance of His promise.

In that, He sooner ceased to be God than to break His promise. However, as far as it goes this was not done with the thought of possible failure on God's side. Neither was it intended to make his declaration more certain, but rather to give Abraham and the heirs of promise a deeper impression of the certainty of the fulfilment of His promise. This also provides something tangible for faith to take hold on. The writer expresses it thus:

> . . . God, determining to show more abundantly to heirs of promise the immutability of His counsel, confirmed it by an oath, that by two immutable things, in which it is impossible for God to lie, we might have strong consolation, who have fled for refuge to lay hold of the hope set before us. This hope we have as an anchor of the soul, both sure and steadfast, and which enters the Presence behind the veil, where the forerunner has entered for us, even Jesus, having become High Priest forever according to the order of Melchizedek. (6:17–20)

The two unchangeable things referred to in which it is impossible for God to lie are (1) the *oath* which confirms the blessings to Abraham and the heirs of promise; and (2) the word of *promise*. God has provided faith with the most satisfactory evidence concerning His unchangeable purpose of mercy towards us. Further proof is seen in the fact that a second oath was taken with respect to the eternal priesthood of Christ. The writer says: 'The Lord has sworn and will not relent: "You are a priest forever according to the order of Melchizedek" ' (7:21). This second oath which confirms the priesthood of Christ after the order of Melchizedek confirms that the very foundation of our hope rests on the unchangeable priesthood of Christ.

And by way of comparison, as the High Priest entered the inner sanctuary on the day of atonement with the atoning blood and bearing the names of the twelve tribes of Israel on his breastplate, so Christ has entered into heaven by His own blood having obtained eternal redemption for us: 'Therefore He is also able to save to the uttermost those who come to God through Him, since He always lives to make intercession for them' (7:25). 'For Christ has not entered the holy places made with hands, which are copies of the true, but into heaven itself, now to appear in the presence of God for us' (9:24).

Therefore, in chapter 1, verse 3 Christ is said to have purged or expiated our sins by Himself. In chapter 2, verse 17 His incarnation is said to have been necessary in order for Him to be a merciful and faithful High Priest in things pertaining to God to make reconciliation for the sins of the people. In chapter 3, verse 1 He is called 'the High Priest of our profession', that is, He is the High Priest whom we acknowledge. This title suggests or gives a powerful inducement for Christians to continue being rooted and built up in Him and established in the faith.

The High Priesthood intimated that God was offended by man's sins and would not have direct or favourable intercourse with mankind. However, because He was disposed to be reconciled to man He chose the means by which to confer His saving grace on them that believe. Thus the vicarious nature of Christ's sacrifice and intercessory ministry answers to all our needs in approaching God and, although the finished work of Calvary brings us into a full and free forgiveness, we still remain sinners disqualified from fellowship with a Holy God. Thus the Heavenly ministry of our Lord answers the further need in that although through His sacrifice on earth we have forgiveness of sins, through His heavenly priesthood we are kept in fellowship with God.

In the light of those great truths the writer commences the practical portion of his epistle with the fact of our confidence to enter into the very presence of God by the blood of Christ. I am in no doubt that our access to the throne of grace is by virtue of the complete work of the Lord Jesus Christ. This is probably one of the most profound truths of the New Testament era. In Ephesians 2:18 Paul writes 'For through Him we both have access by one Spirit to the Father'. In 3:12 he continues: 'In whom we have boldness and access with confidence through faith in Him'.

That which was the peculiar privilege of the High Priest under the old economy of law has now become, through Christ, the privilege of all believers. It is this access to the throne of grace that the writer calls 'a new and living way'. It is the way of approach to God prepared by the sprinkling of the blood of Jesus which enables those with a sincere heart of true worship to have access into God's presence. In Hebrews 9:11, 12 the writer puts it this way: 'But Christ came as High Priest of the good things to come, with the greater and more perfect tabernacle not made with hands, that is, not of this creation. Not with the blood of goats and calves, but with His own blood He entered the Most Holy Place once for all, having obtained eternal redemption.' The holy place which Christ entered is Heaven itself, to appear in the presence of God for us, and as a sure sign that his work was perfect as well as completed, the writer says: 'But this man, after He had offered one sacrifice for sins forever, sat down at the right hand of God' (10:12). Under the law the High Priest was not permitted to sit down in the most holy place, but rather his posture was one of standing, which indicates that his work was not satisfactory. For the blood of goats and calves could not expiate nor propitiate divine justice because his work was ceremonial and not moral. But Christ, 'when He had by Himself purged our sins, sat down at the right hand of the Majesty on high' (1:3).

The veil which covered the entrance to the inner sanctuary of the tabernacle, and later of the temple, was a type of the humanity of Christ. In the Gospel of John 14:6 Jesus himself declared this when He said 'I am the way, the truth, and the life. No one comes to the Father except through me.'

Through the sacrificing of Himself upon the cross, His humanity was torn simultaneously with the veil in the temple. The veil, which hides the inner sanctuary for the gaze of men, was indicative of the fact that the presence of God was not yet accessible to worshippers. But by an act of divine providence it was torn from top to bottom and so it was with the anti-type, Christ. The prophet Zechariah spoke of this when he wrote:

> Awake, O sword, against my shepherd, against the man that is my companion, says the Lord of hosts. Strike the shepherd, and the sheep will be scattered; then I will turn My hand against the little ones. (13:7)

Isaiah also wrote:

> Surely He has borne our griefs, and carried our sorrows; yet we esteemed Him stricken, smitten by God, and afflicted. But He was wounded for our transgressions, He was bruised for our iniquities; the chastisement for our peace was upon Him, and by His stripes we are healed. All we like sheep have gone astray; we have turned, every one, to his own way; and the Lord has laid on Him the iniquity of us all. (53:4–6)

Fellowship with God is not possible without the punishment of sin. Therefore the Father by a judicial act made Christ our substitute; thus he became sin, and God the Father punished our sins in Him.

Therefore, since we have these precious truths we are encouraged; no matter what our personal circumstances may be, or race for that matter, we all can 'draw near with a true heart in full assurance of faith' for '*God shows no partiality*. But in every nation whoever fears Him and works righteousness is accepted by Him' (Hebrews 10:22; Acts 10:34, 35). I believe to 'draw near' is the same exhortation as 'come boldly unto the throne of grace'. The fact that we have been reconciled to God through Christ should lend itself to give us

148

boldness and confidence when we approach God in worship. In all their rituals and religious exercises Israel was privileged to draw near only to that which was emblematic of God's favourable presence in the inner sanctuary. But under the grace-dispensation, we can draw near in the full assurance of faith and the true spirit of worship, having the knowledge that our hearts have been purified from sins and purged from the harmful influence of an unbelieving heart.

Thus, with our minds and hearts enlightened with the truth, we can have genuine fellowship with God with the confidence that Christ our Heavenly High Priest has secured our salvation and has bodily passed into heaven by his own blood, whereby proving the perfection of his atoning sacrifice and the efficacy of his intercessory ministry. And as our forerunner, he has gone before us to prepare the way that we also, one fine day, will likewise enter in a similar manner into heaven.

In the Gospel of John, Jesus tells us 'I go to prepare a place for you. And if I go and prepare a place for you, I will come again and receive you to myself; that where I am, there you may be also' (14:2, 3). Furthermore, as the great High Priest over the spiritual temple (Church) and by virtue of his eternal priesthood, all acceptable worship is committed to his management. Thus the reality and efficacy of Jesus' work gives us a full satisfaction in our conscience as we execute our priestly function in offering up spiritual sacrifice unto God. On the other hand, if our heart is burdened and polluted with the sense of unpardoned guilt, it will render us totally unfit for fellowship with God. Such conditions make it impossible to have a solid ground of confidence towards God.

The spirit of fear is as much a spoiler of a confident trust as is jealousy. So let us be mindful of the fact that whatever prevents us from drawing near to God will also disqualify us from Christian service. For this reason many Christians have become ensnared by mere reflex worship brought about by unsound religious impressions. It goes without saying, that worship which has no foundation in the Word, or inspired by the new life principle of the Spirit, is mere 'will worship'

149

inspired by bodily appetites. It is sad indeed to see so many Christians caught up in a false sense of spiritual security, simply because they interpret Scripture by their experience rather than interpreting their experience by Scripture. When the former approach is applied it will invariably lead to the kind of worship which the Bible calls 'will worship'. But when the latter approach is applied believers will be able to 'prove what is that good and acceptable and perfect will of God' (Romans 12:2).

There is no other ground of acceptance apart from 'having our hearts sprinkled from an evil conscience and our bodies washed with pure water' (Hebrews 10:22). Sprinkling here means the application of the finished work of Christ to the heart by the Holy Spirit, whose ministry it is to bring about spiritual regeneration in the heart. Here regeneration is likened to the washing of our bodies with pure water. But this process is not without our active involvement. For John says 'If we confess our sins, He is faithful and just to forgive us our sins and to cleanse us from all unrighteousness' (1 John 1:9).

Our age of moral and spiritual decline makes it all the more urgent to heed the exhortation to 'hold fast the confession of our hope without wavering'. Whatever may be the difficulties, danger or suffering, we must hold firmly to the doctrine of Christ, 'For we do not have a High Priest who cannot sympathise with our weaknesses, but was in all points tempted as we are, yet without sin' (4:15); and again, 'Therefore He is also able to save to the uttermost those who come to God through Him, *since He always lives to make intercession* for them' (7:25). Although He is highly exalted, Christ is a partaker of our nature and He is, therefore, both capable and disposed to take an interest in all our concerns. For when He was on earth He was subjected to the kind of trials and temptation to which we are exposed, hence He has both the nature and moral capacity to sympathize. Therefore, in His capacity as High Priest He is able to sympathize as well as help us in our afflictions, which arise from being Christians.

To be capable of sympathy it was necessary that He should become man that He might be capable of suffering, and that through suffering He might be capable of sympathy. Therefore, He was tempted in all things so far as His conformity to us was possible. Yet, although His conformity was extensive, He was not completely like us. For, although He was made in the form of sinful man, yet He was without sin. Therefore, His trials and temptations did not arise out of any personal guilt or depravity on His part. Nevertheless, He was tried in all the ways which are suited to the human nature and capacity whilst He was engaged in the performance of His Father's will. In contrast, however, our trials and afflictions are sometimes the direct result of our own disobedience to God's will.

Hence the writer of this epistle could say:

> For such a High Priest was fitting for us, who is holy, harmless, undefiled, separate from sinners, and has become higher than the heavens, who does not need daily, as those high priests, to offer up sacrifices, first for His own sins and then for the people's, for this He did once for all when He offered up Himself. For the law appoints as high priests men who have weakness, but the word of the oath, which came after the law, appoints the Son who has been perfected forever. (7:26–27)

Here lies the important distinction between Christ's heavenly priesthood and the earthly priesthood according to the Aaronic order. For they, being sinful human beings, were obliged to offer expiatory sacrifices for themselves as well as for the people whom they represented. But Christ, though He was exposed to human weakness and afflictions did not need to offer sacrifices for Himself, because He was absolutely innocent and indeed perfect. Therefore, being unfettered with any thought of any kind of weakness in our Lord's mediatorial ministry, 'let us draw near in the full assurance of faith by a new and living way which He consecrated for us, through the veil, that is, His flesh'. Amen.